MacGregor Basketball Series

DEFENSIVE DRILLS

EDITED BY BOB MURREY

Volume
13

MacGregor Sports Education
Waukesha, Wisconsin

© 1987 by

MacGregor Sports Education

All rights reserved. No part of
this book may be reproduced in any form or
by any means, without permission in writing
from the publisher.

Library of Congress Cataloging-in-Publication Data

```
Defensive drills.

   (MacGregor basketball series ; vol. 13)
   1. Basketball--Defense.  2. Basketball--Coaching.
I. Murrey, Bob.  II. Series.
GV888.D44   1987        796.32'32       87-4180
```

ISBN 0-941175-14-6

PRINTED IN THE UNITED STATES OF AMERICA

CONTENTS

1. DIAGNOSTIC DRILLS *Lou Carnesecca* 5
2. DIAGNOSTIC DEFENSIVE DRILLS *Lou Carnesecca* 11
3. PROGRESSIVE DEFENSIVE DRILLS *Ron Billings* 19
4. FUNDAMENTAL DRILLS FOR MAN-TO-MAN DEFENSE *Bill Foster* 26
5. MAN-TO-MAN DEFENSIVE DRILLS *Bob Donewald* 30
6. DEVELOPING A SOUND MAN-TO-MAN DEFENSE *Eddie Sutton* 37
7. DROP BACK DEFENSE *Jim Martin* 47
8. DEFENSE *Denny Crum* 54
9. KEY HOLE DEFENSE *Darrell Hedric* 58
10. FUNDAMENTAL DRILLS AND TEAM DEFENSE *Gerald Myers* 62
11. DRILLS FOR PRESSING DEFENSES *Bill Mulligan* 66
12. MAN-TO-MAN DEFENSE *Dick Parfitt* 72
13. TEACHING HARD-NOSE MAN-TO-MAN DEFENSE *Gene Bess* 86
14. REDSKINS DEFENSE *Jerry Pimm* 90

1
DIAGNOSTIC DRILLS
Lou Carnesecca

We began thinking about what was beating us. It was 1) 1-on-1 drives 2) uncontested layups 3) easy hoops for not boxing out 4) not playing the screen properly and 5) not stopping the break.

One thing is important. These drills must be run with care. They tell you so much. You only need 3 or 4 players. They tell you who's not afraid to mix it up, who will get loose balls. Besides having defensive values, it makes practice more lively. A player can't say, "He's not my man." He can't say, "It's mom's fault." We must teach the dangers of foolish fouls. They put points up. They put good players on the bench.

To show on- and off-ball responsibilities, 2 doesn't hand off. 2 cuts behind to a help position (Diagram 1)

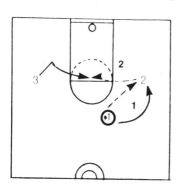

Diagram 1

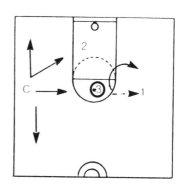

Diagram 2

3 guards 1. Coach moves around to see if 2 is aware of ball and man. (Diagram 2)

You can now vary what you do. You can channel to help. You can make the jump shooter extend himself. 2 looks to help and recover. 3 must box out. (Diagram 3)

All go for a rebound on a miss. We call no fouls in this drill. We're on the road.

There are 3 keys to a good defense; 1) play the ball tough 2) make the next pass difficult 3) jam.

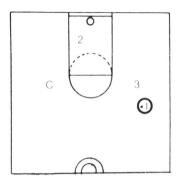

Diagram 3

1-on-1 from the middle (Diagrams 4-6)

We can pass left also.
1 gets in help position.

2 takes handoff.

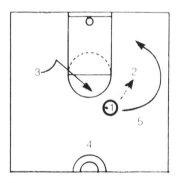

Diagram 4

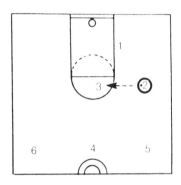

Diagram 5

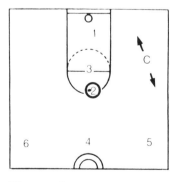

Diagram 6

3 on defense.

Shout instructions to 3 for help.

On a score make them all do it again or on miss make all go to board again.

Be sure ball handler waits for defense to assume position.

Screening Drill (Diagrams 7-11)

We cover these situations in this drill:
- over the top

DEFENSIVE DRILLS

- in-between
- hedge
- switch
- double team

Over the top

1 sets screen.
4 comes up and call pick.

1 picks again as 2 comes back—we are working over the top.

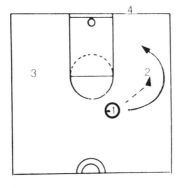

Diagram 7

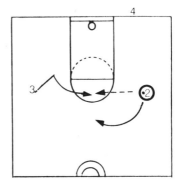

Diagram 8

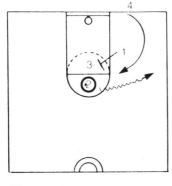

Diagram 9

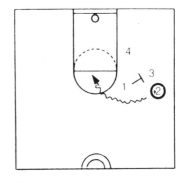

Diagram 10

No easy hoops is the underlying theme! If the man gets free we check and go get it. The kids are diagnosing their own ills in these drills. Note: the defense straightens up to get over the top of screens.

- **in-between (be sure to push the man through)**
- **hedge**
- **switch**

I believe sometimes you have to switch. Hope you can force the dribbler away and put pressure on him. We front the roll man and yell "help" to the weakside. The screener's man is the one to call

"switch" or "stay." Tell offense not to pick up dribble; keep the ball alive. Truly great teams are simple and execute well.
- **double team**
  Don't use this until late in the year. Use against high picks.

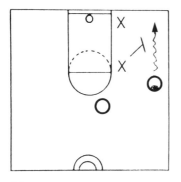

If dribbler gets to baseline and must turn back, we double team.

Diagram 11

Beat to the Spot—looking to force man coming across high and wide (Diagrams 12-17)

2 takes offensive position.

Diagram 12

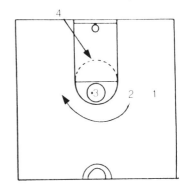

Diagram 13

Clair Bee said success was a combination of material, coaching, and luck, with material being 65%-75% and the other two equally divided.

You need talent to be a big winner. Losing can be good at times. It makes you improvise. You get the most out of yourself. Anybody can coach after a win. You must be up after a loss. Get them up!

Don't be too hard on your kids. Anyone can lose their poise. We lost a World Championship because of it when I was with the Nets. We were down one and had the ball on the side against the Indiana Pacers. We set this up.

DEFENSIVE DRILLS

3 on defense 4 should maintain line off the ball if 2 moves up and down.

If 2 comes across, 4 gets his elbow in the way but keeps it close to his own body.

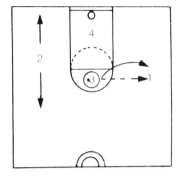

Diagram 14

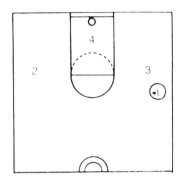

Diagram 15

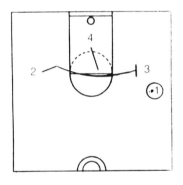

Diagram 16

If 2 can't post up, he comes up to pick on 3.

Rick was wide open. His defensive man fell down. The great Rick Barry, one of the greatest ever to play this game, had a wide-open 12 footer. He lost the ball off his thumb.

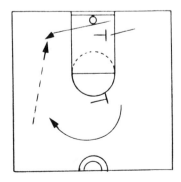

Diagram 17

Stopping the Transition (Diagrams 18-19)

Get up on rebounder who passes ball in.

1 now overplays 3 trying to force him high and wide. 2 shoots if 3 goes backdoor and is covered. 1 must box out.

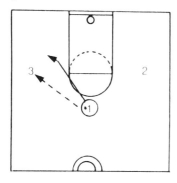

Diagram 18

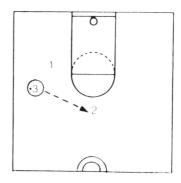

Diagram 19

We do these drills everyday (15 minutes total each day). We combine the drills as the season goes on (7-8 minutes).

2
DIAGNOSTIC DEFENSIVE DRILLS
Lou Carnesecca

The object of these drills is to help you improve your man-to-man defense by incorporating these three and four man drills into your daily workouts.

Rather than emphasize basic individual fundamentals like stance and foot position, these exercises deal with various defensive problems and assignments.

These drills will cover how to defend the one-on-one moves; how to overplay; how to handle screens, and finally, how to beat the man to the spot. We will also be able to key on boxing-out and also react from offense to defense, and vice-versa.

In a short time these drills will enable you as a coach to diagnose your players' defensive weaknesses and then make the necessary connections.

Since you are working with three and four people per drill, you can easily identify the error and correct it immediately. The drills are flexible in that you don't need the whole team; you can work with three or four or with part of the team. Alternate two of the four exercises into your daily workouts for about 10-12 minutes a day, and by doing this you will be preparing your player both mentally and physically for most defensive maneuvers. You will also be able to check the quickness and aggressiveness of your player and those who are prone to commit costly fouls.

RULES OF OPERATION

1. In the 3 man drills (E.Q., one-on-one from side and middle) ball is kept alive until someone scores. The, next three on line start drill. The offensive man has to always beat two defensive men, e.g., one man on the ball, other defensive man in help position.
2. In the *two-on-two* (e.g., screen and beat to spot) if offense retrieves their own rebound, they continue playing until they score. Should defense either steal or stop offense from scoring, next group on line starts. Drill Again.
3. Make sure that defensive players are set before offense starts its moves.

4. Coach calls all fouls, and in the beginning dictates whether offense should drive or take jumpers, so as to zero in on the particular phase of defensive play.
5. In the beginning, I would suggest that you don't call fouls, but after two weeks, when defensive players commit a costly foul, have player repeat the drill in order to make them aware how costly fouls can be.
6. At the coaches discretion, any time offense scores, the coach can make player repeat drill, until defense successfully stops the offense.

One-On-One: Side

Basic set-up: 1 with the ball is at the top of the key, while 2 and 3 take positions at the foul line extended. (Diagram 1)

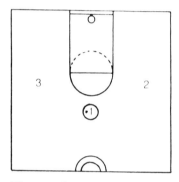

Diagram 1

1 passes to 2 and goes behind 2 and takes an offensive position on the side of the court. As 1 is passing to 2, 3 fakes baseline and comes to the foul line area to receive a pass from 2; after 2 passes to 3 he cuts around 3 and takes a help-slide defensive position in the lane area. (Diagram 2)

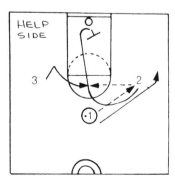

Diagram 2

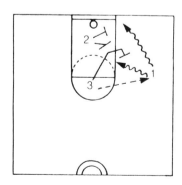

Diagram 3

DEFENSIVE DRILLS

With 2 in a helping position, 3 passes to 1 and goes to cover him defensively, 1 can either drive right or left, with 2 helping out should 1 get by 3. Remember: 1 should not start his offensive moves until 1 and 2 are read defensively. (Diagram 3)

One-On-One: Middle
Same set-up as one-on-one from the side. (Diagram 4)

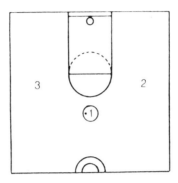

Diagram 4

1 passes to 2 and goes around 2 taking a defensive position in the foul lane area looking to help out. 2 passes to 3 breaking to the foul line. 2 after his pass goes behind 3 for hand off. 3 hands 2 the ball and is ready to play him defensively. (Diagram 5)

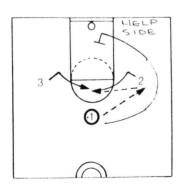 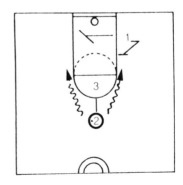

Diagram 5   **Diagram 6**

2 can either drive right or left, or take jump shots off the move. If 2 gets by 3, 1 is ready to help out. (Diagram 6)

Overplay: one-on-one
Basic Set-up: (Diagrams 7–9)

In all these set ups 1 can either start his play to right or left.

1 passes to 3 and goes directly behind 3. 3 after passing to 2 coming to the foul line area, turns around and takes a denial defensive position on 1.

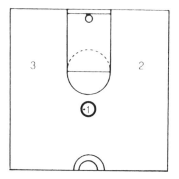

Diagram 7

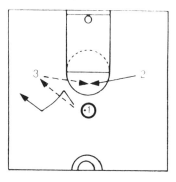

Diagram 8

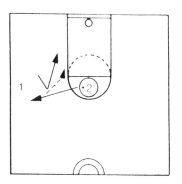

Diagram 9

As 2 starts to dribble toward 1, 3 denies the pass and, should 1 go back door, 3 opens up looking to steal the pass from 2.

DEFENSIVE DRILLS

Beat to Spot: Two-on-Two Drill (Diagrams 10-12)

Same exact basic set-up as the screening drills depending on where the first pass is made. 4 always goes away from the 1st pass made.

Same diagram as one-on-one to the side, except in this diagram, 2 goes off 3 and takes an offensive position on the weakside. Now 4 having a ball and man in sight steps into the foul line area to play.

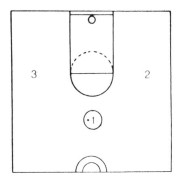

Diagram 10

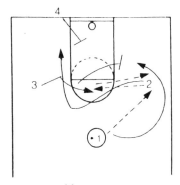

Diagram 11

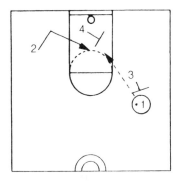

Diagram 12

Again 3 plays 1, but we key on defending 2 coming across for an easy pass or establishing a strong pivot position. Again, 4 had dual responsibilities, he must defend 2 but must be ready to help should 1 get by on the drive.

Screens: Two-on-Two (Diagrams 13-15)

Basic Set-up:

Same set up as one-on-one from the side and the middle, except that we add another player 4 out of bounds on the end line area.

1 passes to 2 and goes around 2 to set a block at the foul line extended. 2 passes to 3 and goes behind 3 to receive a hand-off. As this last action is occurring 4 comes up and takes a defensive position on 1 shouting pick left.

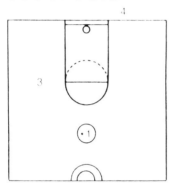

Diagram 13

Diagram 14

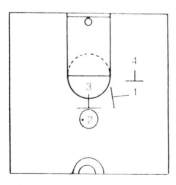

Diagram 15

In this diagram we are now set to work on the various screening assignments: 3 plays 2, and 4 plays 1 setting the pick. 4 being the back calls all the defensive instructions such as over-top, switch, etc.

Over the Top (Diagram 16)

3 playing 2 gets *over the top* of the screen set by 1. 4 helps in pushing 3 over the screen. Getting *over the top* is especially important when playing a very good jump shooter close to the basket.

DEFENSIVE DRILLS

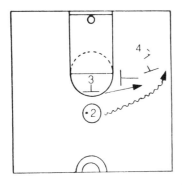

Diagram 16

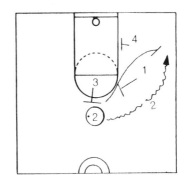

Diagram 17

Switch (Diagram 18)
Whenever 3 is picked off by the offensive move, 4 should switch aggresively to 1, and as soon as 3 is picked off, he should fight to get around front of 1 to avoid the mismatch.

In-Between (Diagram 17)
In this maneuver 4 steps back and pushes 3 through. We like to use this move whenever 2 is a poor outside shooter, or when 2 is outside his shooting range.

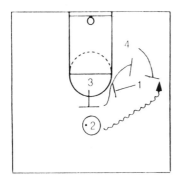

Diagram 18

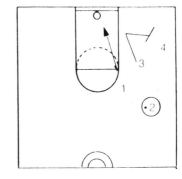

Diagram 19

Continuation of the Switch (Diagram 19)
Here 4 who switched plays 2 aggressively to put as much on 2 to avoid an easy pass to 1 rolling to the basket. 3 with his hands up high front 1 rolling down.

Hedge (Diagram 20)

Whenever 4 sees that 3 is late playing the dribbler, he jumps out in front of the dribbler to delay or stall until 3 catches up to 2. Again, we do this to avoid the mismatch.

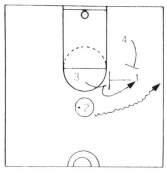
Diagram 20

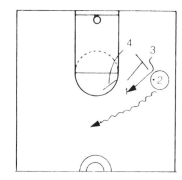
Diagram 21

Reverse Dribble to Repeat Dribble (Diagram 21)

In all of these screening maneuvers, if the defensive man has defended well, the offensive man 2 can reverse dribble and come off the block set again by 1.

3
PROGRESSIVE DEFENSIVE DRILLS
Ron Billings

Drills Chair
A. Work in pairs have one sit in chair the other behind. When the man in chair is ready palms up we pull chair out.
B. Shuffle drill back to chair—slide into chair.
C. Start practice with chair—end—practice with chair.

Instance
A. Defensive position (Diagram 1)
   Teach with the use of the chair
   1. Sit down position
   2. Feet wider than legs, width of chair
   3. Back straight
   4. Palms up
B. Never change lead foot from chair. Stay the same. Split crouch—Ball side/Help side
C. Ball—you—man (Diagram 2)
   1. Flat triangle
   2. Defensive man one step of base to ball
      Anticipation: Drill

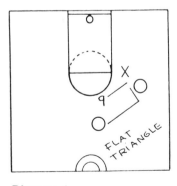

Diagram 1

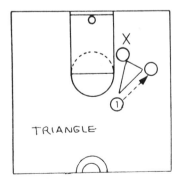

Diagram 2

Basic Drill/Flat Triangle

Diagram 3—Basic Drill/Ball on Floor
1. Walk around the circle
2. Ball can be any place
3. Defense walk to different spots on floor
4. Walk for ball-you-man-flat-triangle
5. Stance
6. One step off base

Walk around drill-coach with ball-move to different place.

Diagram 4—Flat Triangle. Walk around coach with ball-two players.
1. Ball-you-man
2. Defense two jumps toward ball for flat triangle
3. Stance chair-keep low

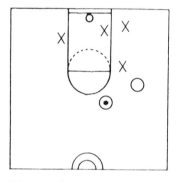

Diagram 3

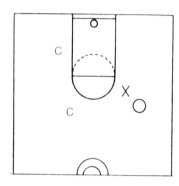

Diagram 4

Diagram 5—Post Defense, Walk around, Four players.
1. Coach can be either place
2. Flat Triangle
3. Post defense rules
   - The ball is above free throw line extended, we defense him from top.
   - The ball is below fit extended, we play base side.

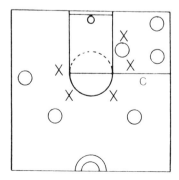

Diagram 5

DEFENSIVE DRILLS

Diagram 6—Post Defense.
1. Bring post across
2. Check defensive position at each spot
3. Post break across defense beat him across deny post ball or high post
4. Defense man on stand tall-stance

Diagram 7—Perimeter pass situation
1. Defense players jump 2 steps to ball and then get in their Flat Triangle
2. Guards seal off helps on Hip-switch
3. Guards: automatic switch on split of high post

Diagram 6   **Diagram 7**

Diagram 8—Triangle Drill Live, First line drill, Offense Free Lance.
1. No switching
2. 3 on 3
3. Stance-Flat Triangle help recovery over top
4. First live drill
5. Offense passing game rules

Diagram 9—Four on Four Halfcourt live-two coaches on baseline/Wooden Drill. Rule-Define stick man.

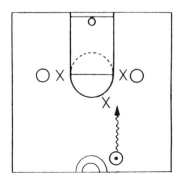 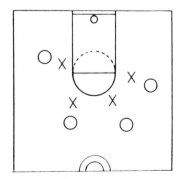

Diagram 8   **Diagram 9**

1) Pressure on ball. 2) Make offensive man 2nd dribble hollow pressure offensive man *turn into middle*
1. 15 minutes a night
2. Insist on rules
3. Tough on ball
   - jump with pass
   - help recovery
   - flat triangles
4. Two coaches on baseline talk to players
   Man-to-Man rules-remind
5. (After shot) Rebounder-block out—step right into the crotch of the shooter
6. Constant-correction
7. Keep ball if you score

Drill: Help and Recovery
Diagram 10—Add the Post
1. m/ to c/ to f-1 drive to base
2. Post jam center-cause traffic
3. x-1 must stop f-1 driving to basket
4. f-1 stops pass back to c to f-s

Diagram 11
5. x-1 gets back to his man. Post block x-1 getting back to f-2
6. x-1 approaches with slide hand on ball

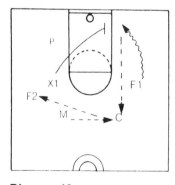

Diagram 10

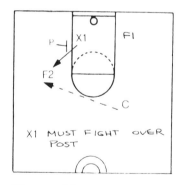

Diagram 11

Drill: Teach Aggressiveness
Diagram 12
1. Coach rolls ball on floor when ball gets to free throw line player 1-2 after it. Whoever gets the ball is offense. The other is defense.

DEFENSIVE DRILLS 23

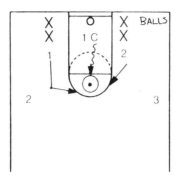

Diagram 12

Drill: Loose Ball Drill

Diagram 13—Coach now calls basket 1-2-or 3.
Defensive player must get there and stop the offense player. Take charge, don't foul.
Diagram 14—Two-One Offensive Rebounding
   1. Rebound-2 gets it-1-3 players on defense power move it up.
   2. Coach can pass direct to 1-2-3.
      Other two on defense.

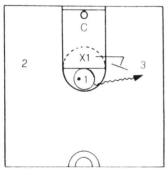

Diagram 13 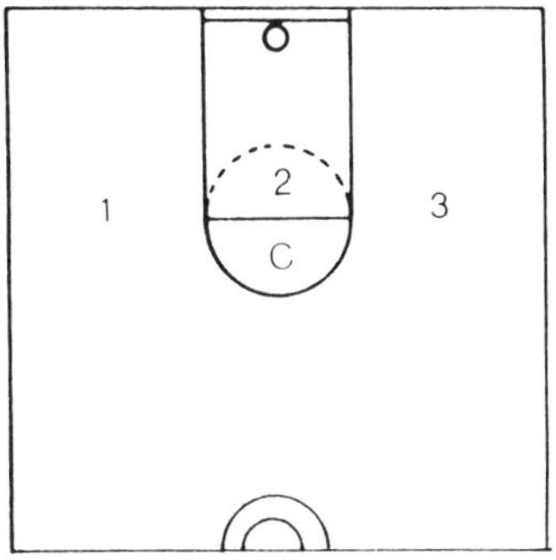   **Diagram 14**

Diagram 15
   1. C pass to #2
   2. #2 drive to basket. #1 must get there take charge.

Drills: Help & Recovery

Diagram 16
   1. x-1 deny pass to F breaking to help.
   2. Forward breaks to basket x-1 must open and stop pass to F.
   3. x-1 must flash as f-2 comes to high post.

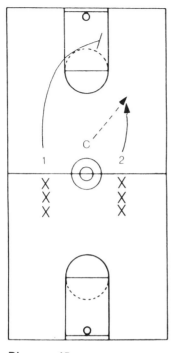
Diagram 15

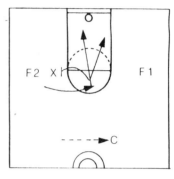
Diagram 16

4. Don't be concerned about lob, pass to f-2. This pass can't be made during regular game situations.

Drill: Help Recovery
Diagram 17
1. x-1 calls flash-deny HIP
2. x-1 stops baseline put numbers on f-2
3. f-2 pass back to f-1 hip
4. x-1 must get back-stop shooter
5. Block out

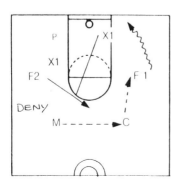
Diagram 17

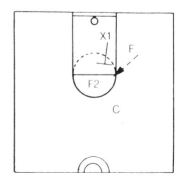
Diagram 18

DEFENSIVE DRILLS

Diagram 18
   6. Note F-2 must shoot-can't drive

Drills Seventy percent of drills for Defense for first two weeks.

Four-Four.

5 minutes for this drill. Rotate position to the right every man plays each defense position.

Diagram 19
1. Offensive man 2 is allowed to make pass to 4 drives base line, beat man. X-3 Defensive man has to get over and help, put the numbers on 4 stop him.
2. X-1 rotates to pick up open forward
3. Emphasis on ball.

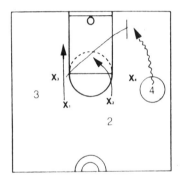

Diagram 19

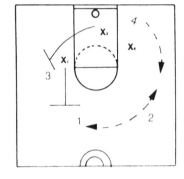

Diagram 20

Four on Four Rotation-Defense

Diagram 20
1. Defense X-s. Stops 4-4 reversed ball back out to 2.
2. 2-pass to 1.
3. Defense X-1. Must recover to his man.
   Play 4 on 4.
4. X-3 must get to his man.
5. 3/4 quarter speed to walk in early of practice sessions.
6. Double team on baselines between X-3 - X-4.

4
FUNDAMENTAL DRILLS FOR MAN-TO-MAN DEFENSE
Bill Foster

Before I get into my topic of defense I want to tell you a couple of things about my philosophy. Games are won by good defense. Everybody likes to shoot, you never ride by playgrounds and see kids practicing sliding drills. Defense is not that popular, but teams that win championships play good defense. Any of the final 32 teams could have won the national title. Talent is so good now that the team that plays the best "D" wins. All of the final four teams played different styles of defense. They all played good "D" though. We led the ACC in scoring one year. We were also second in defense. Some coaches think good defense is holding the ball and keeping the score low. They then think they are a heck of defensive team—not true. We shot every 15 seconds—could have had a 20 second clock and it would never go off. The thing we try to sell our players on is success. Success for some teams may be 10-10. It depends on a lot of things other than winning. If winning was the only thing—Kentucky was the only successful team in the nation. They were the only team to win their last game. In our case, we were very successful. If winning was the only thing, I would be unemployed and many of you would be too. We are successful if we can finish a game, come into the locker room and look everybody in the face. If we feel like we did everything possible to win the game, then we were successful. You can work only so hard and so can the kids. You are crazy to think you can get 100-110%. If you get 75% you're doing well. No matter what the score is, if they did everything they could, you were successful. Work hard and pull together. We played on even keel all year. That's what it's all about. All of us can't win the conference, make All-American, etc. But the thing is, if you did your best you were successful. I tell our guys, success is a journey, not a destination. If you ever think you are already there someone will beat you. It happened all year in college ball. The day of the undefeated college team may be over.

We try to sell our kids on three things: 1) attitude. "Six inches between the ears." Your altitude will be determined by your attitude.

DEFENSIVE DRILLS

You aren't going any higher than your attitude will let you. I would rather have great people and good players than great players and good people. You have to have good people to do anything outstanding in life. If you have enthusiasm you can do anything. Enthusiasm is caught and not taught. Don't ever base everything on winning and losing. If you do, you'll never be successful. There'll be times when you'll lose, I don't care who you are—I see teams doing things exactly opposite from the way they are taught, but they are successful (like the guy with the awful golf swing that shoots par and the man with the pretty swing that can't play a lick). Team. We have these two words on our practice shirts—attitude and team. They are also on the walls of our dressing room. Those two words are very important—you have to have a team play or if you have a player that is a good shooter, you must tell him to compliment his teammates for good passes, etc. If not, that ball will go inside or somewhere else. They must be a team. Team meetings are good, but you must deal with individuals—team play is a must.

We run break down drills for 2 to 3 weeks before getting to shell and possession drills. Shell Drill—divide into 3 teams—4 on 4 drills with 5 on each team (divide as evenly as possible).

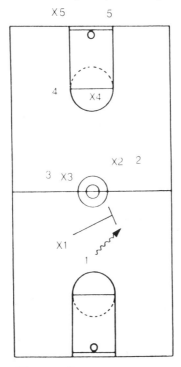

Diagram 1

1. 5 possessions and rotate from free throw shooting to offense to defense.

2. Points:
   - all fouls are one shot opportunities.
   - all jump balls go to defense.
   - all jump balls go to defense.
   - turn-over goes to defense.
   - offensive charge to defense.
   - defensive rebound to defense.

   All stop the possession.
3. Offense
   - score.
   - offensive rebound another opportunity to score.
4. Five in or one after 2nd possession, etc.
   (cheering and coaching)
5. All jump balls go to defense—offensive foul counts as point for defense.
6. Run this drill from
   100-full court
   75-3/4 court
   60-little more than 1/2 court
   40-little less than 1/2 court
7. You can start this drill from out of bounds (sideline or baseline).
8. If you are on post, you can only be in post area 2 seconds.
9. Normally we use this drill in about the middle of our practice.

We give an award for "shell defense"—shell team award. We have 3 teams—4 men on each team. Have competition all year. Our guys would rather win this award at the end of the year than any other award. Shell drills—they are on same team all year. We have t-shirts made up with their team on it. They love to compete in this drill. They kill each other and really get after it. It helped us build our defense this year. They never get tired of it. You have to sell defense. We use our defense to score.

Transition is what it's all about. Our guys play hard. We've beaten teams by 40 points and I've gotten badly rapped because of it, but I can't call them off. I'm not going to tell them not to score. We get after people.

When we shoot well we aren't bad. But the defense determines how well you do. You need to play good team defense. The best offensive guy will kill the best defensive guy all day long. So what you've got to do is sell five guys on playing 3 of theirs. Keep good pressure on the ball and get good sagging help on the offside and you can pressure them. Guys with good average speed can play good man-to-man defense. We break the court down as follows: 40 is the top of the circle. 50 is half court. 75 is 3/4 and then of course, full court. We don't pick up any farther back than 40. If we play a team that is lightning quick we pick them up at the 40. That stops all that transition stuff. My philosophy with a man-to-man defense is

DEFENSIVE DRILLS

don't let them do what they want to do. How good a team is depends on where you pick them up. Once we were playing a team in a tournament in Springfield, Mass. and the scouts closed their books because we forced them out of everything they wanted to do. If they want to go one way make them go the other, etc. You're gonna get scored on; I don't remember any shutouts this year. We tell our guys, "They're gonna score on you." Boys worry about teams going back door. I tell them, "Make them go back door on you." How many of you start your offensive practices going back door each day? I don't. The coming thing in basketball today is not with the guards but with the high post. That's the toughest place in basketball to defend.

Possession Defense-(start about the third week). Can be run from 100, 75, 60, 40, and out of bounds (sideline) or after made free throw.

WAYS YOU CAN SCORE

Offense
1. if they score (5 pts.)
2. offensive rebound (2 pts.)
3. fouls plus they keep the same possession.

Defense
1. deflection (1 pt.)
2. missed free throw (1 pt.)
3. force T-over (2 pts.)
4. fast break off basket T-over (5 pts.)
5. defensive rebound (1 pt.) score on break (5 pts.)
6. take charge (3 pts.)

You get five possessions, then the same team goes to offense and offense to defense. The loser runs two line drills, while the winner gets a water break. The drill starts with one team shooting a free throw.

5
MAN-TO-MAN DEFENSIVE DRILLS
Bob Donewald

Defensive Philosophy
1. There is nothing new in what we do. We have developed our philosophy and style after talking with some of the great defensive coaches in the country and studying their styles.
2. We only play a man-to-man defense and do little switching or pressing.
3. Our teams are not known for their quickness or jumping ability.
4. We feel the three most important factors for playing good defense are:
   - A thorough understanding of how to play individual and team defense.
   - Adequate preparation in every aspect of individual and team defense.
   - Hard Work!
5. We break our squad up for most defensive drills:
   - All squad members work on every defensive drill.
   - With certain drills major emphasis is our forwards and centers.
   - With certain drills major emphasis is given to our guards.
6. We believe that to play our type of defense, we must work at it every day—all season long. We use individual and team defensive drills from the first day of practice to the last. We start every practice with a defensive drill.
7. We feel it is necessary to spend a considerable amount of time on defense for the following reasons:
   - Players develop a basic understanding of how to play individual and team defense.
   - They develop the necessary skills.
   - They develop the necessary timing.
   - We have time to prepare them for any and all situations that might arise during a game.
8. When we start playing games, we want our defensive play to be more advanced than our offensive play.

DEFENSIVE DRILLS

Defensive Drills

We put a manager in front of the entire squad. He either points to or calls the direction they are to move. They will move one step or three steps (determined by coaches).

Points of Emphasis (Diagram 1)

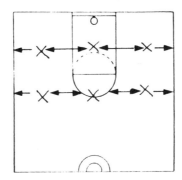

Diagram 1

1. Feet should be shoulder width apart in a staggered stance.
2. The back should be basically straight with the player bending at the knees.
3. Forearms should be parallel to the floor with the palms of the hands up.
4. The player's first step should be made with foot closest to direction he wants to go. Step should be made quickly and his foot should stay as close to floor as possible.
5. Move quickly and stay low.

We want to deny all penetrating passes. We have all of our players learn to deny the offensive man the ball from forward position. We use a stopwatch and have players deny ball for 10-21 seconds. Once offensive man receives ball, drill is over. A manager tries to pass ball to 1 as x1 tries to deny pass. (Diagram 2)

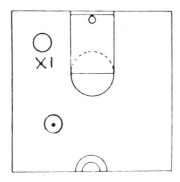

Diagram 2

Points of Emphasis

1. Have defensive man position himself so that his extended arm and his head are in passing lane.
2. Palm of hand on extended arm would be open to the ball.
3. Hips closed, feet in a staggered position and slightly wider than shoulder width.
4. Head in a position so that he can see his man and ball.
5. If his offensive man back-cuts, x1 should allow 1 to go two steps before "1" opens to ball and retreats to basket.
6. Do not allow your players to lunge for ball unless they *know* they can steal pass.

Although we emphasize denying penetrating passes, we are just as concerned that the defensive man is in a good defensive position and ready to play good one-on-one defense once his man receives the ball. Once the pass has been thrown to their man, our players are taught to either go for the steal or jump to baseline side of their man and be ready to play good defense. We put a mark 8' above baseline. We want defensive man to prevent baseline drive by the time offensive man reaches mark. If offensive player drives to middle, defensive player forces him to go away from basket. To teach this concept, x1 is in good contesting position on 1. 1 breaks toward 2 and 2 hits him. As ball is being thrown to 1, x1 jumps to baseline side of 1. (Diagram 3)

Diagram 3

Points of Emphasis

1. Must pressure ball once his man receives pass from 2.
2. X1 steps first with foot closest to direction 1 is trying to drive.
3. If 1 drives to middle—do not give him a direct route to basket—force him to go wide. First step is key—step toward opposite corner of ten second line.
(Diagram 4)

When a defensive man is guarding a man with ball and offensive man passes defensive player jumps to ball. 2 pass to 1. 2 then cuts off

DEFENSIVE DRILLS 33

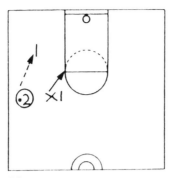

Diagram 4

Jump to the ball.

1 for return pass. X1 is guarding 2. As 2 passes to 1, x1 jumps off 2 to prevent return pass.

Points of Emphasis

1. The defensive man must jump as ball is being thrown; he must not wait until his man cuts.
2. When defensive man jumps to ball, we want him to open his hips so he can see both ball and his man.
3. The defensive man must be between ball and his man.

Over the Top (Diagram 5) We want to fight over top of all picks set within an individual's shooting range. We station two offensive men (without defensive men on them) at sides of free throw line. Defensive man guarding ball must play tight. 2 may pass to 1 or 3 and cut off for a return pass. X1 must fight over top of screen and deny return pass to 2.

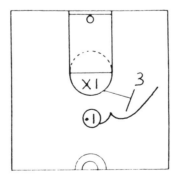

Diagram 5

Points of Emphasis

1. The defensive man must jump to the ball as soon as his offensive man throws the ball.

2. As he approaches the pick he must step over it with the foot closest to it and throw his hips forward so he can slide over.
3. Defensive man must beat offensive man to screen, but we do not want him to go by it until offensive man does.
4. Defensive man wants to encourage offensive man to backcut or cut wide of screen. (Diagram 6)

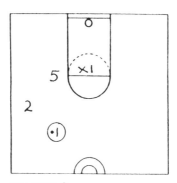

Diagram 6

Guarding the Medium Post

We want to deny all passes to medium post. 1 and 2 do not have defense guarding them. 5 is at medium post with x1 guarding him. 1 and 2 pass ball back and forth—x1 guarding him. 1 and 2 pass ball back and forth—x1 must step around him and deny him ball. 5 does not give any resistance. Once x1 has proper footwork down, we play it "live" and 5 is allowed to "steal".

Points of Emphasis
1. When 1 has the ball x1 is in a deny position. As the ball is passed to 2 x1 steps over 5. X1 should bring his back foot up and move over top and move his front foot back.
2. If 5 steps up to prevent x1 from stepping over top, x1 should quickly slide behind 5 and deny ball from baseline side.
3. When ball is below free throw line, x1 must deny ball from baseline side. (Diagram 7)

We want to deny all passes to low post, as well as to flash pivot. 1, 2, 3 and 4 are stationed around key without any defense. 5 is playing post position with x5 guarding him. Ball is thrown into 5. X5 must deny the ball from 5 at all times. Once 5 receives the ball he will go 1 on 1.

Points of Emphasis
1. Start x5 in a deny position.
2. On all passes, x5 must jump to the ball regardless of what does.
3. X5 must stay between his man and ball at all times, if he is to keep ball away from 5.

DEFENSIVE DRILLS

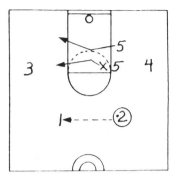

Diagram 7

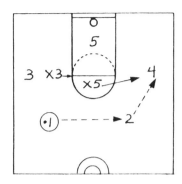

Diagram 8

Pivot Defense

4. Require that x5 play good 1-on-1 defense once 5 receives the ball.
Weakside-Strongside
(Diagram 8) We emphasize weakside defense (side opposite the ball) as much as strong side defense. We feel our players must be prepared to quickly adjust from one to the other. We developed this drill to emphasize importance of changing responsibilities and reacting properly. 1 and 2 look for chance to pass to 3 and 4. 1 and 2 do not have any defense. 3 and 4 are permitted to: (a) break toward ball, (b) flash pivot move, (c) cross. x3 and x5 must: (a) deny their man the ball, (b) help out when his partner is beaten on backdoor cut or is beaten playing 1-on-1.

Points of Emphasis

1. As the ball is passed between 1 and 2, x3 and x5 must jump from deny position to help position, or from help position to deny position. They must jump with ball and not after pass has been made.
2. Once pass is made to either 3 or 4, require x3 and x5 to play good 1-on-1 or 2-on-2. (Diagram 9)

We do not want the ball to be penetrated on dribble between 2 defensive players. We set this drill up in both a guard-to-guard situation and a guard-to-forward situation. 1 has the ball—drives between x1 and x2. X2 must prevent 1 from driving between them and recover to his man if 1 should pass to 2. We do not want 2 to have an open shot.

1. Limit what guards can do offensively: (a) Allow 1 to drive all way for a lay-in or for pass to 2 jump shot. (b) Allow 1 to drive all way for a lay-in, pass to 2 for jump shot, or drive to basket. (c) Allow 3 to backdoor as x3 slides over the prevent split.

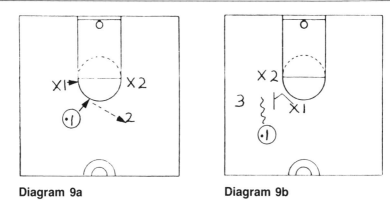

Diagram 9a   Diagram 9b

Prevent the Split

2. Footwork is important—defensive player must step with foot closest to direction he want to go.
3. When 1 passes to 3 require x3 to recover to 3 quickly.
4. If offensive player backdoors the split, x3 should drop his outside foot and retreat to the basket.

6
DEVELOPING A SOUND MAN-TO-MAN DEFENSE
Eddie Sutton

Things I believe you must do to become a good coach:
1. Coach your personality
2. Develop a philosophy for the game of basketball.
3. Attend as many clinics as possible—be a student of the game.
4. Work hard. There are no shortcuts to success.
5. Be enthusiastic.

My Defensive Philosophy
1. First—because I played for one of the great defensive coaches (Mr. Iba), I was convinced that you can't win championships unless you play on the defensive end of the floor.
2. No team sport can consistently win without great team defense. Offense will vary from night to night.
3. You measure defense with the spread of points.
4. You control tempo of the game with defense. We play man defense 80 to 90% of the time.
5. Playing more than one defense poses problems for the opponent. I play zone some of the time, but I'm convinced that man to man is the best defense.

Selling Defense
1. You must spend time on defense.
2. We give awards for defense only. We give the "WOLF MAN" award for taking the charge.
3. Convince your players that anyone can learn to play defense—I believe this.
4. Some players just do not have offensive skills.
5. Sell the parents on how important defense is.
6. Defense wins championship.

General Rules
1. Pressure on the ball.
2. Pressure with ball one pass away.

3. More than one pass away sink to middle—most important is the helper.
4. Force low percentage shots.
5. Control the defensive boards.

Individual Defense
1. Stance—boxer stance—makes no difference which foot is forward—Don't use hands until you learn to use your feet and keep position.
2. Know where the man you are covering and the ball is at all times. If you lose sight of your man, go to basket.
3. When covering more than one pass away sink to middle.
4. Quickness and alertness—Stay down even if away from the ball.
5. React to pass immediately.
6. Never let a man come down the heart of the land—This is "NO MAN'S LAND".
7. Never trail a man to the basket.
8. Talk on defense.
9. If ball penetrates heart of defense—collapse on post in the lane.
10. Don't foul carelessly.
11. You became a defensive player once your team mate releases the ball.

Diagram 1
Alley drill, buddy drill *Explanation*—Offensive player dribbles ball at an angle about 1/2 to 3/4 speed. Defensive player works on proper foot movement, proper body position, etc.

Diagram 2
Stop and Go *Explanation*—Offensive player drives ball down floor in straight line. Defensive player lets offensive man get one step lead and then sprints hard to get back in front. Defensive man should get back down in proper defensive position and stance as soon as he gets back in front. Same procedure is followed the length of the court. Do this drill on the out of bounds lines on the side.

Diagram 3
Taking a Charge *Explanation*—This drill is run the same way as the "Buddy dribble" drill. Offensive player dribbles at angles while defensive man works to keep proper position. In this drill when contact is made defensive man learns to hit the floor on the seat of his pants and recover quickly to his feet.

Diagram 4
Guard to Forward "Contest"—*Explanation*—Defensive man should always contest pass to his man when ball is one pass away and his man is on free throw line extended or below.

DEFENSIVE DRILLS

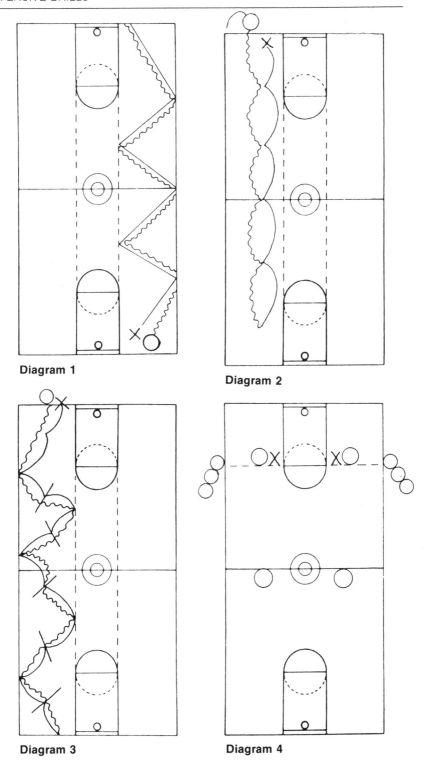

Diagram 1

Diagram 2

Diagram 3

Diagram 4

Diagram 5

"Hog" Drill-*Explanation*—This is a 5 on 5 situation with emphasis on forcing a jump ball. When the defensive player forces the man with the ball to pick up his dribble or the coach could yell "hog" to pick up dribble. Then all people cut off the passing lanes to force a jumpball. Remember-you must see man and ball at all times when you pressure. If you are one pass away, contest player and the ball. If you are two passes away, open up and play one step off line between your man and the ball and you should be in the lane. ALWAYS PLAY BALL-YOU-MAN! Challenge drill, going up with shot with both hands!

Diagram 6

Clear out-Defensive Drill *Explanation*— In this drill the coach or manager takes the ball on the dribble at the forward. When the forward sees the guard coming, he clears out with the defensive forward in a closed stance until the offensive forward reaches the lane, then the defensive forward opens up to the ball, then the offensive man flashes into the post position on the ball side and the defensive forward must learn to defend in the post area on the ball side.

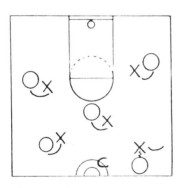

Diagram 5

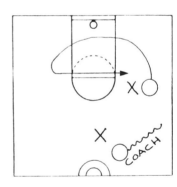

Diagram 6

Diagram 7

Contest G-F pass and deny flash post. Defensive forward contest G-F pass, then offensive guard passes to weakside forward, defensive man should open up to ball and then offensive forward flashes to either a low post or high post position and the defensive man must deny him the ball at both positions.

Diagram 8

Help and Recover Drill—You can start teaching this drill at first by not letting the offense dribble, but the idea is to let the offense any place on the floor have a two on one situation, the offense dribbles hard at the goal and about at the free throw circle area pitches the ball to the other offensive player. The objective is that the defensive man makes the dribbler pick up the ball (help) and when the offensive dribbler

DEFENSIVE DRILLS

Diagram 7

Diagram 8

pitches the ball to the other offensive player, the defensive player (recovers) to his original man and closes on ball.

Diagram 9
Over the Top Drill—On this drill, we place two people-one on either side of F.T. line just outside the circle and a one on one situation out front. The dribbler goes either way to rub the defensive man off on either screener, the defensive man must play basic tough defense on the dribbler, nose on ball, stay low, heels apart, etc. When he sees the screener, he must stick his leg through over the top of the screen, arch his back, stay thin over the screen and stay with the dribbler. Each man goes on defense until all four players take their turn. Rotate to the right.

Diagram 10
Hedge Drill—You start this drill the same as you do over the top, but now we have a 3 on 3 situation. When the ball comes over the screen and the defensive man is beat, the other closest defensive man steps out with his back foot across in front of his own man and tries to get the dribbler to: 1) charge you, 2) pick up his dribble, 3) change direction, or 4) force him to the sideline. Then recover back to his own man.

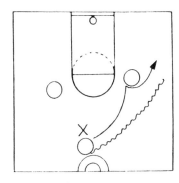

Diagram 9

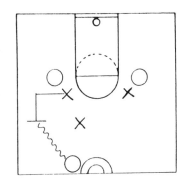

Diagram 10

Diagram 11

Sucker Drill—on this drill the offense passes to a coach in the free throw line extended area. On the pass the defense jumps off to the ball (one step to the ball) in a good low defensive stance. The offense should try to cut to the ball but the defense must seal the cutting lane or front the cutter and make him go to low post area, then the cutter must try to post up in the low post area, but the defensive man must deny him the ball on the ball side or front him if he is at low post if there is help from weak side. If no help from weak side and ball is F.T. line and above you play with over play pressure on ball side. If ball is being passed into low post area with no help from weak side when ball is below F.T. line extended you play the low post base side, ball side.

Diagram 12

Stationary Shell Defense—This is a 4 on 4 drill with the defense letting the offense pass the ball on the perimeter. On every pass, the whole defense should jump to the ball, with the **BALL-YOU-MAN** principle kept in mind. But the main objective is to keep a protective shell around the scoring area. You must keep in mind whether the ball is one pass away or two passes away.

Everyone should know where their ball is, what your relationship between your man and the goal is and know where your man is, so we have a BALL-YOU-MAN philosophy. If the ball is two passes away, you should be one step off a line between your man and the ball, and opened up to ball so you can see your man and the ball. If the ball is one pass away, you jump toward the ball in a good defensive stance. How close you stay to your man when he doesn't have the ball depends on how quick he is in relation to your quickness and how determined you are to play tough defense. Later we will let the offense move around and put in our passing game rules.

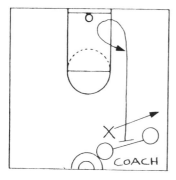

Diagram 11

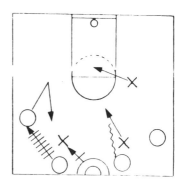

Diagram 12

DEFENSIVE DRILLS

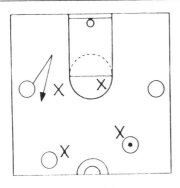

Diagram 12 cont'd.

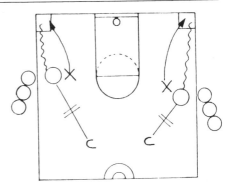

Diagram 13

Diagram 13
1 on 1 Containment—Defense contests guard to forward pass, but allows offensive wing man to catch the ball. When offensive man receives the ball, defensive man shades the offensive man 1/2 man toward midcourt to force him into the box in the corner. Offense rotates to defense and defense rotates to the back of the line on the opposite side.

Diagram 14
Man Drills—1 on 1 with help—Players form three lines at half court and weave to positions as shown in diagram. Player #1 defends player #2 and player #3 is in a defensive help position on the weakside. The ball starts with 2, then goes to 3, to 1, and passes it back to 2.

Diagram 15
Deny the Flash Pivot—Same movement as 1 on 1 with help. However, player #3 is an offensive player flashing across the lane, player #1 defends against the flash pivot, denying a pass from player #2, who has the ball.

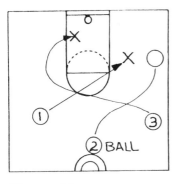

Diagram 14

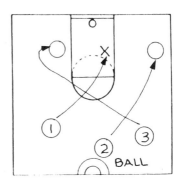

Diagram 15

Diagram 16
Weakside Block-off—Same movement as the other 3 man drills, except #2 shoots the ball, #1 blocks off on #3, an offensive rebounder on the weakside.

Diagram 17
Pivot Defense (low post, ball side)—In this situation, offensive man starts in low post position. The coach has the ball in the 6 hole. The defensive man plays up-hill on offensive man discouraging a pass by placing his hand nearest the ball in the passing lane. As the coach dribbles the ball to the 5 hole the defensive man must move over the top of the man to front him.

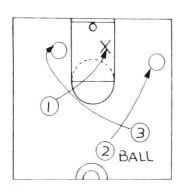

Diagram 16

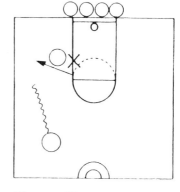

Diagram 17

Diagram 18
Pivot Defense—This is a continuation of the drill above. The coach has the ball in the 5 hole. As the low post man moves away from the ball to the weakside, the defensive man loosens up and maintains a position x (2) near the middle of the lane where he can see the ball and his man. If the post man flashes back to the ball side the defensive man must prevent the pass as in position x (3).

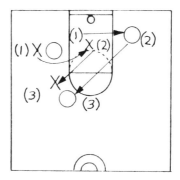

Diagram 18

DEFENSIVE DRILLS

Diagram 19
Guard Switch—This is the only time switching is allowed. When a guard interchange is made above the top of the key, each defensive man must yell "switch" and step out to obstruct the offensive man's path.

Diagram 20
3 on 3 Half Court—Three lines are formed as shown in the diagram. The outside lines should be in the free throw line extended area and the middle line at the top of the key. The ball may be started at any position, and the defense must adjust to the position of the ball. The offense observes the passing game rules and the lines rotate after a score or a defensive rebound.

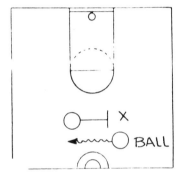

Diagram 19

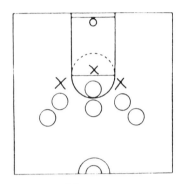

Diagram 20

Diagram 21
Bull in the Ring—5 players are scattered equidistant around the circle and one player is placed in the middle. The offensive players must pass the ball as quickly as possible. The defensive player should fake and drop, trying to intercept a pass. The offensive players may not hold the ball longer than 2 counts and may not pass the ball

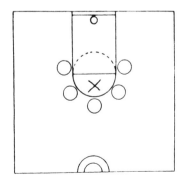

Diagram 21

to a man next to them. If the defensive player touches the ball or the offense makes a bad pass or violates the rules, a new player goes to the middle.

Diagram 22
Head Hunter Drill—The ball starts in the 5 hole. As the wing man throws the ball to the coach, he head hunts the defensive man on the low post man. The defensive man (x1) on the screener (head hunter) must call the screen and loosen up so the defensive man (x2) on the low post may slide through if he is unable to go over the top of the screen.

Diagram 23
1 on 1 Towel Drill—This drill is run on 2 sidecourts. An offensive line forms under the basket at one end, and a defensive player, holding a towel around his shoulder, attempts to play "nose on the ball" defense as the offensive man proceeds down court. When the offensive player gets within 15 feet of the basket, the defense drops the towel and goes 1 on 1. Offense rotates to defense and defense to the back of the line.

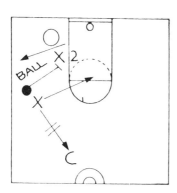

Diagram 22

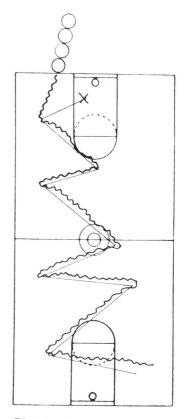

Diagram 23

7

DROP BACK DEFENSE
Jim Martin

DEFENSIVE POINTS

My philosophy is strongly defense oriented and I believe that eventually your drop back defense will do more to win ball games for you than anything.

I. Right to defensive position (see Diagram 1)
   - Some similarity to gymnastics being graded by form-your form will often determine who gets the foul
   - Baseline position; you must get in front of your man, drop back a step if necessary.
   - Must watch that first step when defending the driver; drop back so that he doesn't get the corner on you.
II. Squaring up in front of the shooter (see Diagram 2)
   - Must take defensive stance as squarely in front as possible; then move up toward shooter with little rapid shuffling steps.
   - Both arms should be extended straight up.
   - Jump with shooter only after you have established good position; it is often better to hold that tight position on the floor, forcing shooter to lose concentration because he cannot follow through without bumping into you.
III. Step in front so that you are facing away from him, don't allow him to meet the ball.
IV. Take the ball side away from driving guard. (See Diagrams 4 and 5)
   - This will help avoid being rubbed off on high post.
   - Will hinder guards efforts to set screen for forward.
   - If he goes inside for lob pass, it is a poor gamble for them.

OFFENSIVE POINTS

V. Squaring up to shoot
   - Work at squaring up and put the ball up as quickly as possible.
   - Should try to receive the ball low.
VI. Using guards who have good height and good character.
   - Character and intelligence determines ability to concentrate.
   - Character will determine their leadership ability.

VII. Offenses geared to getting everyone shots and allowing for continuity.
  • My best teams are my most patient teams.
VIII. Delay Fast Break (Diagram 6)
  • Affords good rebounding
  • Lends itself well to our offense

DELAY FAST BREAK

IX. Tip two-handed as much as possible.
  • Like using power layup
X. Hustling back on defense
  • So simple and yet so vital
  • Instead of spending time deciding how to have men challenge outlet passes, we might well concentrate on getting defense back.
XI. Using drop step to get inside
  • Use on base line
XII. Demand the respect of your players and that they respect each other.
  • Need a strong conviction of behavioral limitations.
  • Must be able to communicate honestly and sincerely.

DRILLS

I. Defensive position against driving dribbler

Coach passes ball to either line making that person the dribbler. The front man in the other line immediately flashes in to defensive position trying to draw the charging foul.

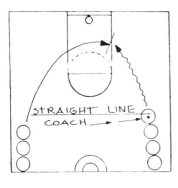

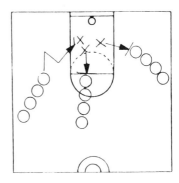

Diagram 1   **Diagram 2**

DEFENSIVE DRILLS

49

II. Squaring up in front of shooter along with rebounding drill.

Ball is passed to any of three lines, and the appropriate defensive man comes out fast being sure to be positioned squarely in front of shooter. The other two men block out their offensive men going to boards.

III. Defensing the flashing post.

Ball is thrown around by 1, 2 and 3, as post man P moves to get open. The defensive man X works to prevent P from being able to receive the ball in the lane area. As illustrated, we give primary emphasis to defense stepping in front of the post flashing into the lane from side away from ball. He is to stay in front of him until he goes above free throw line or outside the lane if he goes low to baseline.

IV. Defensive drill for guards

Set an offensive guard, forward and past as illustrated, each with defensive man. G passes to F and uses a 1-1/2 step and cut

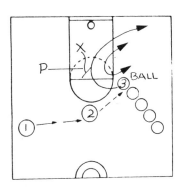
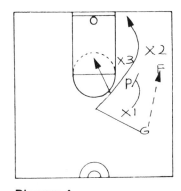

Diagram 3   **Diagram 4**

back move trying to rub off defensive man on forward or post, or he may screen for forward. We like G to move 1-1/2 steps, then try to cut back between X_1 and the ball or cut to basket. Our primary purpose and emphasis is to teach defensive guards to take the ball side away from the guard breaking to basket - X_1 always overplays the ball side. He will open up to ball when G breaks away from the ball.

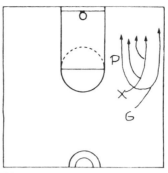

Diagram 5

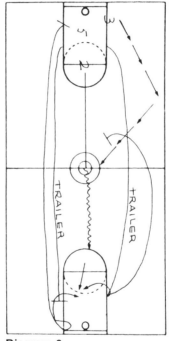

Diagram 6

FUNDAMENTALS OF THE 1-2-2 ZONE DEFENSE

(Advantages of the Zone)
Purposes of Using Zones as Opposed to Man-to-Man
I. PERSONNEL ARE NOT EFFECTIVE MAN-TO-MAN
   • General poor quickness and speed
   • Matchup poorly in height, weight, quickness, etc.
   • Poor man-to-man instincts
II. Double teaming the big men inside is more effective.
III. Often helps to reduce fouls.

DEFENSIVE DRILLS

IV. Forces opponent to shoot outside and takes away their penetration potential.
V. The team that uses both Zone and man-to-man forces opponents to prepare for both and reduces their effectiveness against either.
VI. Changing defenses during a game may have good surprise effects.

WHY A 1-2-2 ZONE

I. Utilizes more man-to-man fundamentals.
   - Requires more reading, thus defense must be alert-can't float and be lazy.
II. Point man takes away guesswork about who picks up ball.
   - Limits penetration down middle and forces ball movement to the side.
III. Lends itself very well to inside double team of big man.
IV. Middle man is not wasted as is often the case in 2-1-2 Zone.
V. Should limit effectiveness of high post.
   - Point man sagging helps keep ball from going to high post man.
   - Some coaches switch from 1-2-2 to 1-3-1 momentarily to cover high post.
VI. Sharpshooter from side (free throw line extended) may be hindered by quickness of front men getting out on him.
VII. Short player is more effective in front of 1-2-2 than on front line of 2-1-2.
   - (Exception: one coach uses the third tallest man at the point.)

WHY MAN-TO-MAN CONCEPTS DETERMINE THE EFFECTIVENESS OF A ZONE DEFENSE

I. Must play solid position defense.
   - Cannot allow man with ball to move toward basket; must take the charging foul.
   - Must not give up baseline.
   - Must step up tight to shooters.
II. Must step in front of men breaking toward the ball in high percentage shooting area.
III. Must lead cutting guards through until someone else is in position to pick them up.
IV. Must pick a man to screen out when a shot is taken.
V. Position to deny pass to post men same as in man-to-man.

It's important that X_1 sets up so as to keep the ball from going into the high post and that X_2, X_3, X_4, and X_5 keep at least one foot in the free

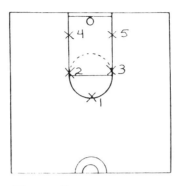

Diagram 7

throw lane until pass is made to side or ball is moved to left or right of top of circle. (Diagram 7)

Wing men X_2 and X_3 are right at ends of free throw line.

Back men X_4 and X_5 will set up at varying depth on the lane depending on the offense; they cannot allow offensive men to flash in between them and wingmen X_2 and X_3.

Basic Shift
Some General Position Responsibilities
FOR POINT GUARD X_1
1. Challenge the ball until it is moved to side.
2. prevent pass into the lane area
3. for offensive high post, sag slightly to keep ball away from him. (This allows wing men freedom to cover the side of the lane area more effectively.)

Low Post Double Team-For Wing Men X_2 and X_3
1. keep hands up and at least one foot in lane when ball is above the circle.
2. jump out to cover wing man who receives pass from point man.
3. if opposite the ball, sag to cover the basket. (weakside lane area)
4. may sag to front low post when ball goes to corner. (Diagram 9)

For Back Men X_4 and X_5
1. ball side man covers man in corner
2. weak side man flashes over to cover strong side of lane (illustrated in basic shift Diagram 8)
3. both must jam lane along with the sagging wing man, that is, they must step in front of man flashing into lane area and force him behind, then open up with arms up to discourage the lob pass.

DEFENSIVE DRILLS 53

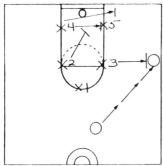 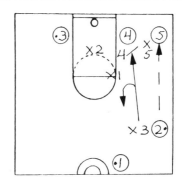

Diagram 8   **Diagram 9**

8

DEFENSE
Denny Crum

Our real forte is our defense. You don't have to spend that much time teaching it. It is very simple to teach. We have five rules.
1. Deny guard—forward, or deny strongside passes. Deny all passes one pass away.
2. Sag hard on weakside.
3. Front all post players.
4. Switch all screens on or off the ball within shooting range.
5. Deny the reversal of the ball.

Let me show you the best way to do those things. First of all, let's take the post. We front all posts. We front three different ways.
1. Half front from the high side with one hand in front and one hand behind. (Diagram 1)
2. Half front from the low side one hand in front and one hand behind. (Diagram 2)

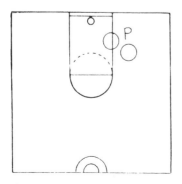
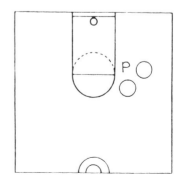

Diagram 1 **Diagram 2**

DEFENSIVE DRILLS

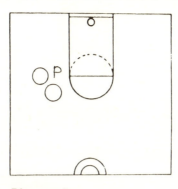

Diagram 3

3. We will full front, facing the defensive man. We do not turn our back to him. (Diagram 3)

We deny the ball strongside, one pass away. We make you go backdoor. We will not let you have the ball for a number of reasons. Most people play a low post offense of some kind. If you have a post player, most offenses are geared around getting that ball into that post. The easiest way to keep him from getting the ball is to keep the forward on the strong side from getting into position to make that pass. It is very difficult for any one person to deny the ball from the post player. Officials will not call the illegal movement of the post. So the most successful way to keep the ball out of the post is to deny the forward the ball in the first place. Once he gets it there, we'll back off of him. He is out of shooting range and we'll take away his offense except for the 1-on-1.

We will sag like crazy on the weakside. Anytime the ball is received below the free throw line we are going to half front from the baseline side.

If the ball is above the free throw line, we are going to half front from the top side.

And as the ball comes down in the area, we are going to slide around to a full front and right around until we are in a half front from the baseline side. Let me show you why we are going to front from the baseline side. We do this because of the help that we will receive from our weakside forward. (Diagrams 4 and 5) I want my defensive forward to be a defensive weakside player. What are you going to do to bring him out of there? (Diagram 6) You are going to bring your weakside player to the high post position. But even then my defensive forward is still only one step away. The forward will still defense the low post man even though his man goes high. He will stay there unless the high post man gets the ball and turns to the basket. Then he moves up to cover. But I don't want that high post to get the ball. I sag my guard to stop the pass to the forward playing the high post. (Diagram 7)

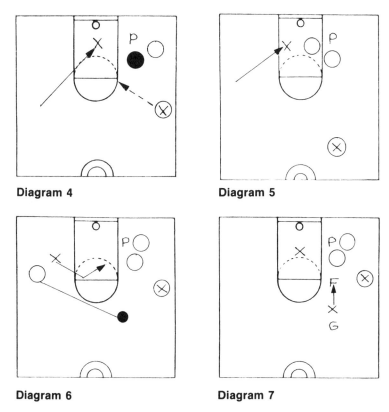

Diagram 4

Diagram 5

Diagram 6

Diagram 7

The key to making this work is when I say we switch all screens. If the offense exchanges on the weakside to keep my defense honest, and if I allow you to bring my weakside forward out with your offensive player, you have done just what you wanted to do. But because I switch on the screen my guard will try to deny the pass to your forward coming back to the top. My forward will stay low when he is screened by your guard. The guard will take the forward. They can reverse all day long and my guard will stay outside and my forward will remain inside. My guard will deny the reversal of the ball by overplaying the man coming high, and the forward will help to keep the ball out of the low post. (Diagram 8)

But if you switch all these screens, you are taking away the shot that they are getting the most. We have talked about switching away from the ball. Now let's cover switching on the ball. (Diagram 9) Let's say that your forward picks my guard. We are going to jump switch and deny the penetration of that dribble off the pick. The same if your center comes out and screens my defensive forward. My center is going to jump switch. (Diagram 10) How many baskets do you score on the screen and roll? It's one of the best plays in the game. But how many screen and roll plays do you score on? You are not going to beat me with the screen and roll.

DEFENSIVE DRILLS

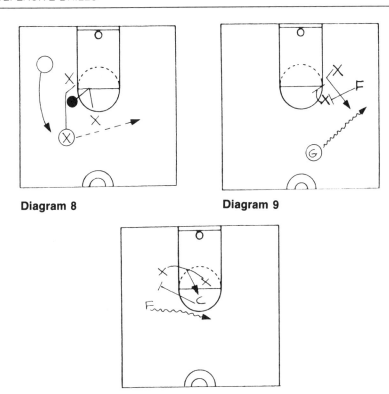

Diagram 8

Diagram 9

Diagram 10

We switch every time. All you have to do is get back and stop the dribble. And then we have the sagging weakside help. So, this defense takes away the jump shot. I buy a scouting report for $35. But with this defense, I don't care what they run. The switching man-to-man will take care of it. I can spend by time much better than preparing for an opponent during my practice time. How long do you spend each week preparing for an opponent? What is more productive? What if I took a player and put him on a spot in which he is going to get his shots during the game and had him shot from there for 30 minutes, or spend 30 minutes shooting free throws? Since I don't care what you run, I don't spend any time in my practices telling my players what you do. That's a real advantage. I think that it is the best.

9

KEY HOLE DEFENSE
Darrell Hedric

The key hole defense is used in place of a zone against a center that we can't control, if we are in foul trouble and are against a team we can't hurdle.

The key hole defense is the same as a pressure defense but we don't deny anything in the perimeter. We are exerting pressure on the ball but we are letting the ball move around the perimeter without any denial from guard to guard or guard to forward. The inside game remains the same, but pressure is exerted on the point of the ball. We don't want any penetration.

Defensive Lead Up Drills
Six Step Drill

Teaches players all phases of defense regardless of his position. A coach has the ball out at top of circle and there are two men in the forward position. (Diagram 1) The defensive man does the following:

- 100% denial of ball-stance is important. We are in a position of overplay.
- Open up-Close down-if man begins to go behind you open up, if he goes back out close down.
- Front the low post-straddle front. The defensive player plays to the side and in front of the man when he goes in low post area.
- Deny on the other side of the floor.

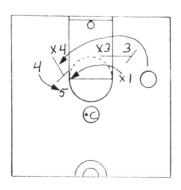

Diagram 1

DEFENSIVE DRILLS

- If offensive man gets the ball on the other side of the floor he (the defensive man) defends the driving lane.
- Rebound.

Diagram 2-Driving lane drill-Guards push the ball sideline then to the middle of the floor where there is help.

Diagram 3-Flash Post Drill-The flash can be a tough action to defend because the offensive man is coming from the help side or opposite side as the ball is coming into the lane. The defender must watch the ball and man in the low post area. As the offensive man flashes, the defensive man forces him *high* and *wide* with his hands up in front of the offensive man.

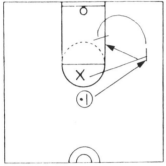
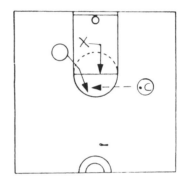

Diagram 2   **Diagram 3**

Diagram 4-Deny the flash post, help and recover on the help side- defensive man takes the offensive man *high* and *wide* with his hands up in front of the offensive man.

Diagram 5-Over the top drill-Point guard always leans the ball sideline. Offensive guard gets as close to the screen as possible. The defensive guard steps into the offensive forward, duck hooks and

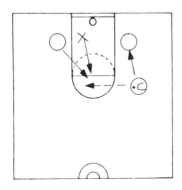

Diagram 4   **Diagram 5**

gets over the top of the screen. On a moving screen the defensive man takes a step behind or hedge move by the offensive man who is trying to screen him.

Diagram 6-2 on 2 defensive moves-The defensive men are working on the step in move, step behind, hedge move and sliding through.

Diagram 7-Defense the following offensive maneuvers:
1. Pass, screen the ball.
2. Pass, screen away.
3. Dribble series behind.
4. Pass, go behind
Communication about screens in this drill is necessary.

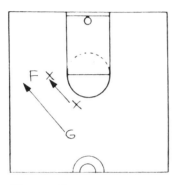

Diagram 6

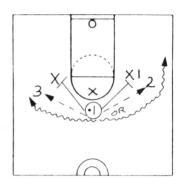

Diagram 7

Diagram 8-Take the Charge Drill-Teaches players how to take the charge. Defensive players should be square to the basket.

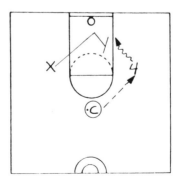

Diagram 8

DEFENSIVE DRILLS

DRILLS FOR POST DEFENSE

Diagram 9-2 on 2 pick down, pick up-Defensive men have to step behind or step in-depending on the pick. No switching is allowed.

Diagram 10-3 on 3 in lane without ball-offensive players move in triangle fashion while defensive men adjust to the situation they find themselves in.

Diagram 9

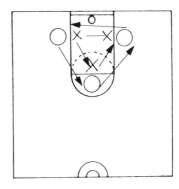

Diagram 10

10

FUNDAMENTAL DRILLS AND TEAM DEFENSE

Gerald Myers

The foundation for any sound basketball team is based on both offensive and defensive fundamentals. Any team has to have good players to win consistently; however, there are some things that can be done to give a team an edge to help them win other than superior material and a home court advantage. That advantage will often come from defense, especially against those teams that do not emphasize defense.

It is necessary that much time be given to the development of individual defensive skills. Fifty percent of our drill time is spent on this aspect of the game. Also both offense and defense are emphasized simultaneously in team situations with at least one member of our staff working with the defense since each offensive move has a counter defensive move and vice versa. This has been a good method in teaching the whole defensive concept that we prefer as well as individual responsibilities in various situations.

The first skills taught early in the year are the basic stance and footwork that we want our players to use both on and away from the ball. This is done through a mass drill in which players are taught a basic boxer's stance, defensive shuffle (approach, retreat, and slide steps), drop step (drop the front foot back when changing directions), cover out (next receiver pressure) and cover back (reverse cut by the offensive man).

The primary objective of defense is to prevent the good percentage shots and to help your team gain possession of the ball without allowing your opponents to score. This can be done by preventing your opponents to pass, cut, dribble, shoot, and rebound at will. These objectives can best be achieved by an aggressive pressure type defense on the ball and a sinking helping defense away from the ball. The following points are the reasons we think a good defensive team gains a consistent edge in winning.

- A strong defensive team is more consistent at home and on the road.

DEFENSIVE DRILLS

- A weak defensive team must perform miraculously on offense to win consistently.
- Defense has the dual role of reducing the number of shots and the quality of shots taken.
- Sound defense will allow a team to control the tempo of the game.
- Defense is a great equalizer.

It is easier to teach an aggressive type defense early in the year and then adjust to a sinking type defense if your players are not physically capable of playing pressure defense, than it is to teach a passive style of defense and then get a team to pressure and become more aggressive.

Since there are many options for the ball handler to use when he penetrates into the middle of the defense, we think it is to our advantage to force everything to the sideline or corner. The highest shooting percentage areas are in the middle of the floor and the lowest shooting percentage area is in the corner and on the baseline.

Any time the player with the ball is in a forward spot, we attempt to influence him or force him toward the corner. We are attempting to force him toward the baseline and take away the inside drive.

Diagram 1. Baseline influence from the forward spot.

The defense influences the offense by over-playing the offense by one half man toward the baseline. The feet are staggered in a heel-toe position with the baseline foot dropped. It is easier to move in the direction of the back foot. We start in this position and adjustments can be made according to the offense man's abilities. On the drive the defensive man must close in and cut off at least halfway from the corner and the basket. Preferably the defense will be able to force the offensive man into the corner. The defense must play close enough to prevent a cross over dribble and penetration into the middle. If the offensive man tries to penetrate into the middle after starting his drive, the defense attempts to keep him parallel to the sideline.

Diagram 1

Diagram 2. Baseline influence with corner help.

The same rules apply with corner help except the defensive forward plays head up with his man instead of cheating one half man toward the baseline. The defensive man in the corner plays next receiver pressure.

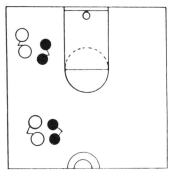
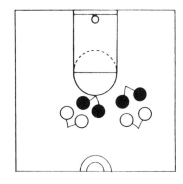

Diagram 2   **Diagram 3**

Any time the man with the ball is in the guard spot, we attempt to force or influence him toward the sideline. In a two guard front the defensive guard influences the offensive guard to the sideline by aligning his outside foot up on the inside foot of the offensive man. The defensive guard attempts to cut the offense off no deeper than the free throw line extended and preferably at the twenty-eight foot penetration line. The weak side guard plays next receiver pressure. This is a closed stance and is taught on all over play situations.

In a guard front the same rules apply except defensive guard influences the offensive man to the side by aligning his front foot between the feet of the offensive guard.

Diagram 3.

The defensive guard influences his man to the side by playing his outside foot aligned up on the inside foot of the offensive man. The weak side guard plays next receiver pressure and is alert to seal off the drive down the middle. This is a closed stance and is taught on all over play situation.

TEAM DEFENSE

Much time and effort must be put into developing team defense away from the ball. Players one pass from the ball play next receiver pressure. They are in a closed stance (hand in passing lane watching the ball over their shoulder), mid point vision, and ready to seal (help) if the defensive man on the ball is beaten in their direction.

Team Defensive Rules
1. One pass from the ball next receiver pressure.

DEFENSIVE DRILLS 65

2. Two passes from the ball-at least one foot in the lane, one hand on their man, and one hand on the ball.
3. Three passes from the ball-both feet in the lane (open stance). Vision is mid-point between ball and their man.

Diagram 4.

G_2, F_4, and C_5 are potential next receivers. The defense on these men play next receiver pressure.

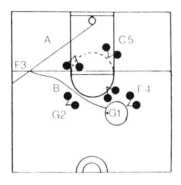

Diagram 4

Weak Side Defensive Rules

1. Two passes from the ball (Diagram 4).
   - Draw imaginary line A through the basket from man through ball forming an acute angle.
   - Bisect the angle, the defensive man two passes from the ball get off his man on angle bisector to a point where mid point vision can be used.
2. Three passes removed (Diagram 5).
   Same rules apply as in (1) except when defense is three passes from the ball, he must have both feet in the lane in an open stance.

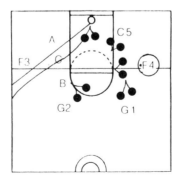

Diagram 5

11
DRILLS FOR PRESSING DEFENSES
Bill Mulligan

Zone Offense

Zone is the most simple offense in the world.
(Diagram 1)
Ballhandler penetrates the zone, goes to the gap and passes to the shooter, who shoots. Everyone else rebounds. Notice rebounders are in perfect position. Keep your offense simple.

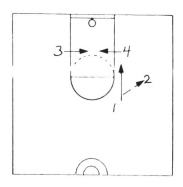

Diagram 1

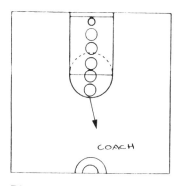

Diagram 2

Attitude Drills

(Diagram 2)
- Coach with ball can:
a. have first player take it away from you.
b. throw it right at his forehead as he moves toward you.
c. throw it anywhere and make him retrieve it.
d. have first two guys square up and throw the ball up in the air. The guy who comes down with the ball is the winner.

These drills tell you immediately who wants to play and builds character. Keep each player out there as long as you want.

We spend much time teaching them fundamentals. We spend hardly any time with our offense or defense. We make our offense real simple.

Drills for Conditioning and Pressing

- **Sit drill**-against the wall. Sit in a chair position for a minute. Practice defensive stance.
- **Defensive slides**-Pair up. Each group has a ball and shuffles back and forth, passing the ball from defensive stance. (Diagram 3)
- **Calvin drill**-Bounce the ball against the wall the length of the court and move laterally. Dribble back.(Diagram 4) Repeat three times.

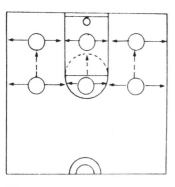
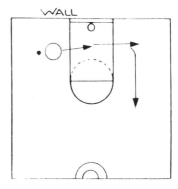

Diagram 3   **Diagram 4**

- **Tips**-Tip the ball against the board and run to the end of the opposite line at the opposite basket. Go for a set time period. (Diagram 5)
- **4 on 2**-O's attack X's 4 on 2-X's attack O's 4 on 2 (need 12 players)-you have 3 groups. (Diagram 6)
- **Bleacher hops**-Hop up the bleachers and walk down. Continuous.
- **Steal from behind**-1 on 1 and 2 on 1-Run up behind a dribbler and steal the ball 1 on 1 and 2 on 1. Several groups go at the same time. Stay low. Tip the ball away, but keep it in bounds.
- **Steal the bacon-transition**-Coach calls out a number and designated players run out and play 1 on 1. (Diagram 7) Coach can call out 2 players or 3 players numbers as a variation. Coach designates a basket before players go out.

Half Court Man Defense

(See Diagrams 8-11)
- **Block Out Drill**-Most important thing in man defense-hold opponents on one shot each time down-use it in every drill-not just a 5 minute period. Guards play catch and when one of them shoots, X1 and X2 must go from ball side to help side as the ball is passed. (Diagram 8)
- **Take the Charge**-We don't compliment the jump shooters-we compliment the players who take the charge.

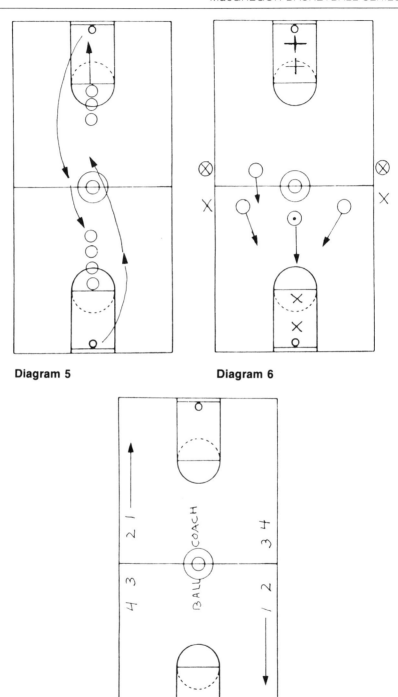

Diagram 5   **Diagram 6**

Diagram 7

DEFENSIVE DRILLS

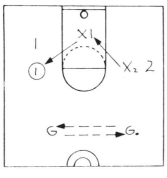

Diagram 8

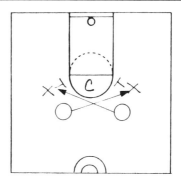

Diagram 9

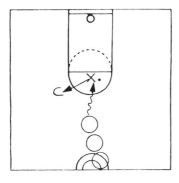

Diagram 10

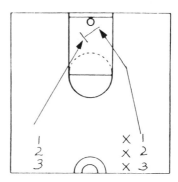

Diagram 11

a. **Post Split**-Pass to post (coach). Players criss-cross. X1 and X2 take the charge. (Diagram 9)

b. **No ball Drill**-X1 guards the coach. When each player comes, he must take the charge from all six offensive players in the line. X1 goes back and guards the coach each time. (Diagram 10)

c. **Full Speed at Half Court**-1 drives to the basket and X1 must get in front and take the charge "chase drill." (Diagram 11)

5 Presses We Have Used With Success
- Man defense at half court
- Man defense at full court
- 3-1-1 full court zone press
- 2-2-1 full court zone press-also rotate
- 1-2-2 3/4 or 1/2 court zone press

Why Press?
We press on made or missed shots. Our reasons for the press include:
- Kids want to play this way.
- Opponents don't like to play against it.

- You control tempo.
- Pressure defenses give you another offense. You can score off your defense.
- You better have some presses-you are not always ahead in the 4th quarter.
- If all presses fail:

You must teach

a. How to foul-dive at the ball and get his arm.
b. Who to foul-foul the poor free throw shooter or foul the new sub.

3-1-1 Full Court Zone Press (Diagram A)

X1 plays on ball and prevents all passes except short one, takes the return pass away. X2 and X3 make sure a man is in front of you. X2 takes 1st pass ball side. X3 goes opposite. X4-ball side prevent pass to mid-court-quickest player. X5-gamble on mid-court opposite-best take the charge guy. All 5 must be in position before ball is inbounded and only X5 has opposite side of floor. Note: Watch eyes of man taking it out; be near a man in your area; most teams will get it in and then attack in same manner. Those who are not organized are sometimes most dangerous. You can adjust to those who are organized.

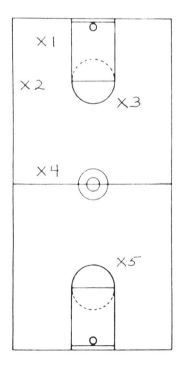

Diagram A

DEFENSIVE DRILLS

2-2-1 Full Court Zone Press (Diagram B)
(Used when opponent gets ball in before we can get our big man back or as a change of pace.) X5-little man, because we press on made or missed shot. We don't care where in bounds receiver goes with the ball, but encourage in bounds receiver to go sidelines. "Soft Press"-kind of token press. "Suicide Press"-hard press change the tempo by changing the way you are pressing between soft and hard press.

1-2-2 3/4 and 1/2 Court Zone Press (Diagram C)
- 2 time ball at 3/4 or 1/2 court
- Key point X3 prevents pass to the middle. If they pass laterally, X3 can come back up.
- More of a bothersome press.

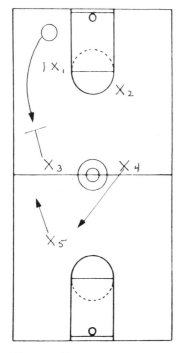
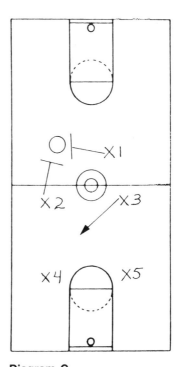

Diagram B   **Diagram C**

12

MAN-TO-MAN DEFENSE
Dick Parfitt

Against Bowling Green we were up by one, but they froze the ball and waited for the last shot and they made it. We called time out with 2 seconds left, 1 point down, and possibly out of the conference championship. During the time out I checked with the scorer and also told the referee near the table we were going to run an out of bounds play that would make their man charge into our man. The play is predicated on them guarding the man out of bounds who will throw the ball in. We instruct the man throwing the ball in to ask the referee loud enough for the defensive man (guarding against the throw-in) to hear: "Ref, can I run the baseline?" The referee said, "yes, you can run the baseline." (after a made basket). We position our men like this (Diagram 1 & 2). One of our players at half court is instructed to be close to the other referee in case we don't get the foul called and we

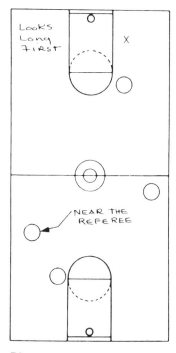

Diagram 1

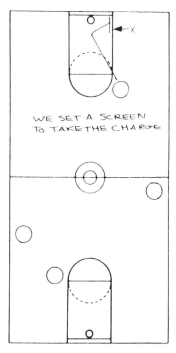

Diagram 2

DEFENSIVE DRILLS

need to call time out. The out of bounds man first looks long to occupy the defensive man in front of him. The man at the foul line moves down to set a screen and our out of bounds man first looks long to occupy the defensive man in front of him. The man at the foul line moves down to set a screen and our out of bounds man runs the baseline causing his defensive man to charge into our screener. We set the screen to "take the charge." The foul was called. Our man went down and sank 2 free throws (after they called time out) and we won by 1 point. Since then we have renamed the intentional foul play to the "Sting."

DEFENSE

At a clinic held by Coach Jud Heathcote in MSU, he mentioned five important points on defense. The topics are his and the ideas behind them are as I applied my thinking to his topics.
1. Understand-teach the defense you understand. I understand man to man and I don't understand matchups very well-not enough to teach and make them do it.
2. Believe-I believe in man to man. If you believe strong enough, you can get it across.
3. Sell-You have to sell your defense to your assistant coaches and to your players.
4. Teach-I try to be very careful about teaching. You've got to be able to teach your defense, for example, to position your people on defense.
5. Demand-demand that your players do it; it's how you get it out of them. You make them play defense. We all have different personalities, we all demand a different way...some do it by substituting.

Coach Heathcote said the ones we really fall down on are numbers 1 and 5.

We start practice at 3:00. I don't like a lot of rules, but certain rules you have to have.

I do not start our practices at 2:39, I can't worry if Dan Roundfield is going to come through the door at 3:00, 3:01, or 3:05. He'd better be in the gym at 3:00 because, I think, you make the rules for your stars. I can't afford the nervous energy of watching the door? Put in a rule, you'll make your coaching more pleasant. If he comes at 3:01 he will not practice that day. He will do a series of sprints and then get out of my sight. "If I had to coach you today you would irritate me. You must not have wanted to practice that badly."

At 3:00 we warm up. (flexibility etc.) At about 3:15 we practice defense (drills etc.) At 4:00 we take a break; a "Chip-aid" break. It's one of the best things I've done since I've started coaching. We socialize for 2-5 minutes. It's the one time in practice they can go and get a drink. They look forward to it and it breaks up practice. At 4:05 to

4:30 we practice offense and from 4:30 to 5:00 we practice offense and defense. Other than running during practice (3:00-5:00) the only other running we do is during free throws. We're a good free throw shooting team and I think it's because of the way we do it-all pressure (individual and team). If he makes it he can go and get a drink while the other guys do their suicides. We are generally done at 5:00 unless a player wants to stay around or we're finishing a game. We scrimmage during pre-season on Wednesdays and Fridays and they know at 5:00 we will be finishing up. During practice especially after warmups we will stop and play a 2 minute game creating "late game situations."

Defensively, we have a set of philosophical rules to govern our thinking:

1. Stop the ball before it gets to the 21 foot area. You have to have a guard that can stop the opponents' guard from penetrating. We used to turn the ball inside.
   Now we turn the ball to the outside.
2. Cut the lead-deny the pass if your man is one pass away.
3. Get a triangle if your man is 2 passes removed. (ball-you-man)
4. Jump toward the ball-as the ball moves, you move in that direction.
5. Catch up to the ball-if it passes you, get down court!!!
6. Stop all cuts to the ball and basket.

DEFENSE AND DRILLS

We now force the ball to the side and we always try to force a team to their left. Take everything to the side and keep the ball from penetrating to 21 feet and into the middle area. (Diagram 3) Against the Miami offense, if they took it to their right side they'd kill us with their cuts off the stack so we pick the ball up high (often full court) and force him to the side and left. (Diagram 4)

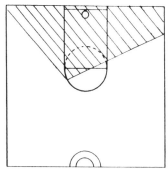

Diagram 3

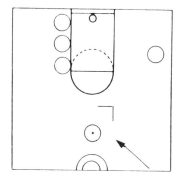

Diagram 4

DEFENSIVE DRILLS

Diagram 3—We now force the ball to the side and we try to force a team to their left. Keep the ball from penetrating the 21 foot area and into the middle area.

Diagram 4—We pick the ball up high (often fullcourt) and force him to the side and left.

As he moves to the side; we do not want him to cut back into the middle-we must be in a position to react and cut off a possible move into the middle from the side. (Diagram 5)

So we keep him on the side and we are facing the side-line and we try to "keep him on the side." (Diagram 6)

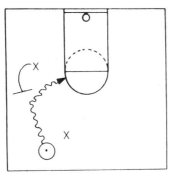
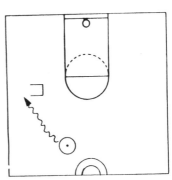

Diagram 5   **Diagram 6**

Diagram 5—We have lost our position facing the sideline and the dribbler can cut back into the middle. We don't want this.

Diagram 6—We try to keep him "on the side" and our position is to face the sideline.

From this defensive position, he could drive toward the baseline and take a jumper but he'd be doing it on the move and under pressure and we would give help to stop penetration but we do not want him to go to the middle-this kills us. (Diagrams 7 & 8)

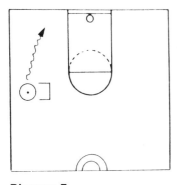
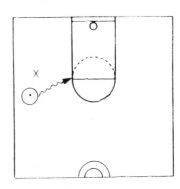

Diagram 7   **Diagram 8**

Diagram 7—In this defensive position he could drive the baseline to take a jumper but we'd get help to stop penetration.

Diagram 8—We do not want him to penetrate into the middle...this kills us!

To stop quick reversals of the ball from the side to the top of the key we play high up on the man and deny the pass. The old way had him sagging in toward the lane to give help against penetration to the foul line area but now our facing the sideline while guarding the ball prevents this (Diagrams 9 & 10) and we play tough on any reversal.

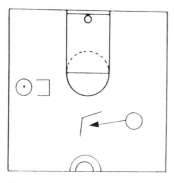

Diagram 9

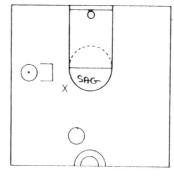

Diagram 10

Diagram 9—Play up high to stop a reversal.

Diagram 10—This old way had us sagging to defend against the drive into the middle but now because of our sideline defensive position we stop penetration and play tough on the reversal.

Drill-One on One

Motion thrives on reversal. Against a one or two guard front we get him to go left and when he's on the side we face the sideline and we are always ready if he tries to come back for the drive into the foul lane area. We shield him out of this area. (Diag. 11)

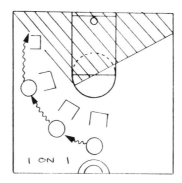

Diagram 11

DEFENSIVE DRILLS

Diagram 11—Against a one or two guard front, we get him to go left and when he's on the side we face the sideline. When he picks up his dribble we attack the ball!

Drill-Two on Two "Clear Drill"

The key rule in this drill is when your man "clears" away you stay on the ball side until the dribbler has been stopped. Then go find your man. When he picks up his dribble, go find your man. How many times has that man who has cleared away received the ball over there from the ball side wing anyway? And remember when the dribble is stopped we attack the ball to make any penetrating pass difficult. (Diagrams 12, 13, 14)

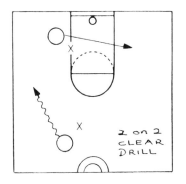

Diagram 12   **Diagram 13**

Diagram 12—Our rule: When your man clears away, you stay on the ball side until the dribbler has stopped. Then go find your man.

Diagram 13—How many times has a man who has cleared received the ball from the wing anyway? And are we attacking the ball?

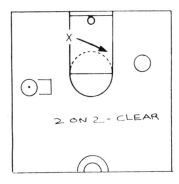

Diagram 14

Diagram 14—find your man when the dribbler is stopped.

Drill-Three on Three

Rule: When you're one pass away, cut the lead. Make the reversal difficult! (Diagrams 15, 16)

Diagram 15
Basic Setup

Diagram 16
Reversal

Diagram 15—Rule: When you're one pass away, cut the lead.

Drill-"Close Up and Triangle Drill" (my favorite)

The coach and manager pass the ball back and forth across to each other. This drill teaches cutting the lead. As the pass is made, one defensive man cuts the lead to his man while the other defensive man is moving quickly to play triangle defense.

(Bobby Knight) getting off his man in the direction of the ball. (Diagrams 17, 18) The man cutting the lead should get his head up in front of the offensive player's body and have his rear foot pointed

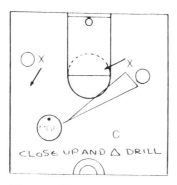
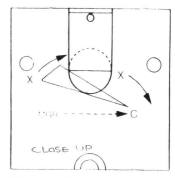

Diagram 17

Diagram 18

toward the basket. We keep yelling "get up!, get up" because they're worried about the back cut. We don't get hurt by the back cut. If we do, we say "don't cut the lead as high."

Diagram 17—As manager and coach pass the ball back and forth, one defensive man cuts the lead while the other gets off his man and plays triangle defense.

DEFENSIVE DRILLS

Diagram 18—The man who cuts the lead gets his head up in front of the offensive man's body and has his rear foot pointed toward the basket.

Drill-Shell Drill

The ball starts in the corner. The offense passes the ball and each receiver holds it for 2 seconds while the defense is learning to a) cut the lead; b) jump to the ball; c) get his triangle. (Diag. 19)

Then we add cutters. From the baseline the coach will point to an offensive man who will pass and then cut and all the defensive men have to adjust to the threat of the cutter. (Diag. 20)

In our pregame warmup drill we have 2 offensive men start on the baseline and 2 defensive men positioned in bounds who guard them and cut the lead as they cut to receive a pass from a manager. The opposite defensive player establishes his triangle defensive position and we play 2 on 2. (Diagram 20)

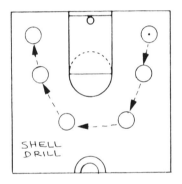

Diagram 19

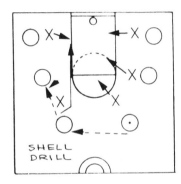

Diagram 20

Diagram 19—(Ball starts in corner) Each receiver holds the ball for 2 seconds while each defensive man is learning to cut the lead, jump to the ball, or get his triangle position.

Diagram 20—Then we add cutters. The man will pass and cut and the defense has to react to the cutter.

Drill-Four on Four-Half Court

The offense freelances and we apply all our defensive rules in this half court situation. (Diagram 21)

Drill-Full Court Pressing Defense

The same rules apply full court. Deny and cut the lead and triangle man can get off his man a little farther if his man is a longer distance down court from the ball. (Diagram 22)

We have been keeping fewer players on our squad. No one wants to be a sub. So in our practices we have 3 teams of players that rotate playing 4 on 4.

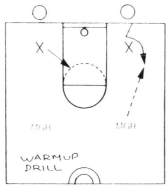
Diagram 21

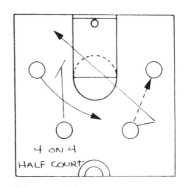
Diagram 22

Diagram 21—One defensive man cuts the lead, the other works to get triangle defense. Then we play 2 on 2.

Diagram 22—The offense freelances and we apply all our defensive rules in a half-court situation.

Drill-Seven Phase Defensive Drill

The first drill is cut the lead. It has 8 cuts by the offensive man and the defense must deny each cut. If the defensive player gets the ball it's one on one. The offensive player sticks to the cuts in the drill, he doesn't freelance. (Diagram 23)

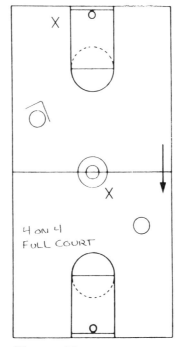
Diagram 23

DEFENSIVE DRILLS

Phase I

"Cut The Lead Drill" (Diagram 24)
- Whenever the defensive player is one pass removed from the ball, he must cut the lead.
- When a pass is made, the defensive player immediately jumps toward the ball while staying one step off an imaginary line between his man and the ball.
- When the offensive player backcuts to the basket, the defender should open up by keeping his back toward his man as long as the offensive player is in the lane.

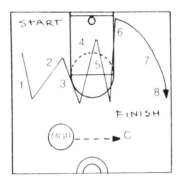

Diagram 24

Phase II (Diagrams 25-28)

1 on 1 From Wing Fig. 1
1 on 1 From Post Fig. 2
- Do not let go base line.
- Force towards the middle.
- Undress him by swinging up viciously at the ball with inside hand.
- Opposite man play defense when come back.

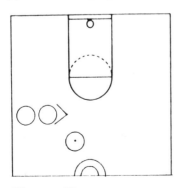 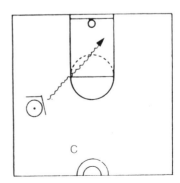

Diagram 25

Cut the lead.

Diagram 26

Position after offense has the ball.

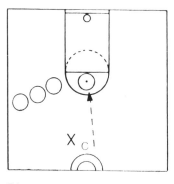

Diagram 27

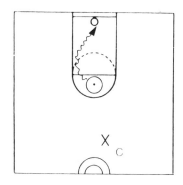

Diagram 28

Force player to his weak side.

Even though the defensive player is playing to the offensive player's right hand, he should still make it tough to drive to the basket and possibly force a bad shot.

Phase III

Diagram 29—Position before offensive player flashes.
Diagram 30—
- Low Post must receive ball in lane.
- Position of defense is "cut the lead" after low post flashes.
- Defense must work to keep flash post from catching ball in lane.

Diagram 29

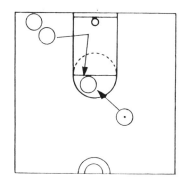

Diagram 30

Phase IV (Diagrams 31-32)

High-low
  Cut the lead.
  Open up—he must pass ball
- Low post must receive ball below dotted line in the lane.
- When low post flashes into the line, the defense opens up by putting his back to the offensive player until he leaves the lane, defense cuts the lead again.

DEFENSIVE DRILLS

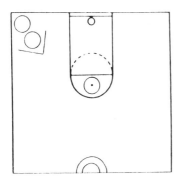
Diagram 31

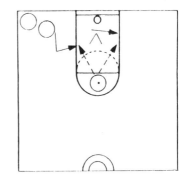
Diagram 32

Phase V (Diagram 33-35)
Reverse Action
- Jump Toward Ball.
- Do not let point guard get the ball back unless he receives it where he is not a threat to the defense.

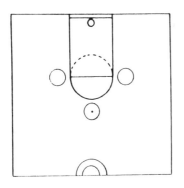
Diagram 33

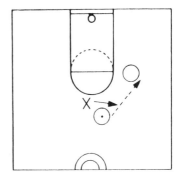
Diagram 34

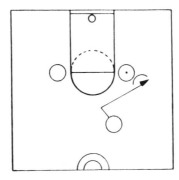
Diagram 35

- If the point guard does get the ball back the defense post man is in position to panic the dribbler.
- Defensive player must go over the top.

Phase VI
Defense Against the Scissors
Diagram 36
- Position of defense to keep ball out of post

Diagram 37
- You jump toward the ball.
- You must switch.
- You must say I got 'em.
- Make the guards run right up your chest.
- Use your inside hand to harass the post man while he has the ball.

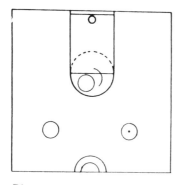

Diagram 36

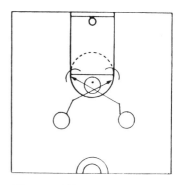

Diagram 37

Phase VII
Tagging Drill
  The defense must step out and panic the dribbler while still staying close enough to tag their man.
  Diagram 38—shows the basic defensive position.

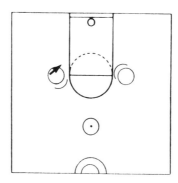

Diagram 38

DEFENSIVE DRILLS 85

Diagram 39—shows position of defense when dribbler goes to his right.
Diagram 40—shows position of defense when dribbler goes to his left.
Diagram 41—shows position of defense when dribbler goes back and forth.

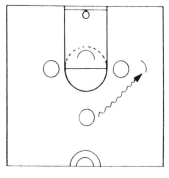
Diagram 39

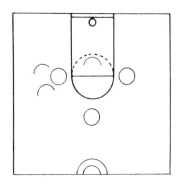
Diagram 40

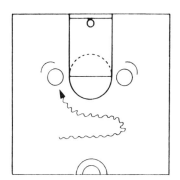
Diagram 41

13

TEACHING HARD-NOSE MAN-TO-MAN-DEFENSE

Gene Bess

If you are going to hold the opponent down on defense, you're going to have to hold the ball on the offensive end. I like pressure man-to-man defense, not necessarily full court, but playing in the passing lanes. We want to control the tempo of the game. We want to dictate to the offense.

What do you want to get done? I want to overplay penetrating passes. I want people to have to shoot from the outside.

Basic 7 Team Defense
1. Stop penetration
2. Overplay guard — forward pass.
3. Eliminate the baseline drive.
4. Deny the pass to the post area.
5. Check all shots.
6. Block off and go on rebounds.
7. Handle all special plays.

Individual Requirements — Defense
1. STANCE — Knees bent and hands up.
2. POSITION — See the man and the ball at all times.
3. HELPSIDE — Key to pressure defenses.
4. LINE OF THE BALL — Get ahead of the ball, this includes chasing dribbler.
5. LINE OF DEPLOYMENT — A must in the defensive post area.
6. REMINDER: 80/20 — EFFORT/TECHNIQUE
    a. Go on the floor after the ball.
    b. Draw charge.
    c. Rebound in the crowd.

DEFENSIVE DRILLS

Stop Penetration Drill
C=Coach
O=Offense
D=Defense

DEFENSIVE DRILLS

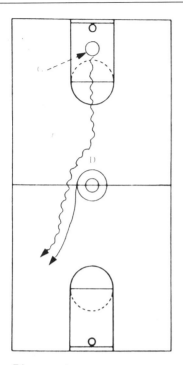

Diagram 1

RULE: Once the offensive player crosses half court, he must be forced to continue in that direction. (Diagram 1)

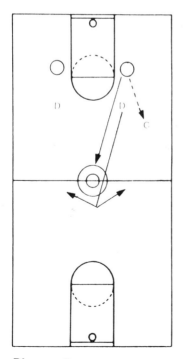

Diagram 2

Show the line of the ball. (Diagram 2)

— 2 on 2
— Offense passes to the coach.
— Offense cuts, defense must get back in the line of the ball.

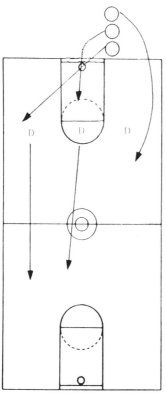

— Coach calls one of D names, he must run forward and touch the end line and then run to catch up.
— Offense goes and it's a 3 on 2 situation until the 3rd defensive man gets back.

Diagram 3

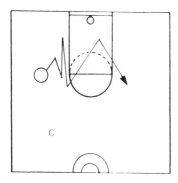

Diagram 4

Practice offensive cuts and the defense of these.

Diagram 5

Line of Deployment.

DEFENSIVE DRILLS

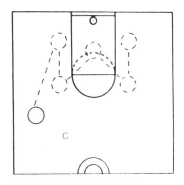

Diagram 6

Dotted circles represent key defensive areas.

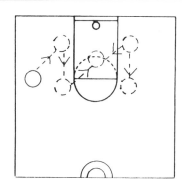

Diagram 7

Angle (>)represents how to play the man in each of the key defensive areas.

POST DEFENSE (Diagrams 8-11)

down the lane and to the corner.

Line Of Deployment

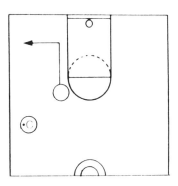

Diagram 8

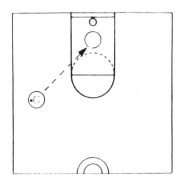

Diagram 9

Defense In Each Position

How To Defense Each

Diagram 10

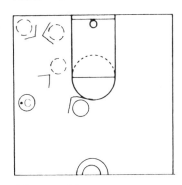

Diagram 11

14

REDSKINS DEFENSE
Jerry Pimm

Defense is one of my favorite topics because I feel the strength of any program is in the defensive end. Before we get into defense, I'd like to put some questions into your minds. In your opinion, what is a good coach? Who do you feel in your area who you compete against is a good coach? Do you consider yourself a good coach? In my opinion, a good coach can make himself successful in a 100 different ways. There's a different formula for each person — for each individual personality.

I think your presentation to those youngsters, the methods you use, and the consistency with which you approach them is the most important part of coaching. In my opinion, a good coach is one who has X amount of people and X amount of talent and gets the most from that talent. He helps each one of those individuals reach a better level of proficiency and then as a team, he gets the potential out of that team. The good coach may not have the greatest win-loss record, he may not be writing books, he might not be as well known as some others, but deep down inside you know that this guy is going to be tough to beat that particular night. And what in your opinion is the toughest thing about that team? In my opinion, it always comes back to do they play hard? Do they play good defense? Do they *really* play with emotion and enthusiasm? Those are the things I think if a coach can get his teams to do, they will reach their potential. They will have fun playing the game. Over the years as I look at people, their programs, how they were reared, where they learned their basketball, people I have a great deal of respect for, and basically it does come back to personality. These people I respect, they could be running coaches, all kinds of tempo coaches — but basically, they are solid people who care about what they are doing, who care about the youngsters they are working with, who get totally involved in those young people — not just in basketball, but totally in their lives. I think the high school coach has much more influence on a life than we do at the college level. They are working with lesser skilled people, sure, but they are working with minds that are being formed and really have a great deal of influence on those youngsters.

Besides winning, what do you want out of your program? Where am I going in coaching? What am I going to do the rest of my life? What are my long-range goals, my short-range goals? Do I want to

DEFENSIVE DRILLS

stay here or go to Florida or the West Coast? Where am I going? We constantly have to re-evaluate our goals. I think success comes to us in many different ways.

In asking yourself questions about defense and when you're developing your philosophy, one must determine what he wants out of the defense. How much time am I going to spend teaching and working on defense?

Diagram 1 — 3 minute slide
1. Retreat to baseline.
2. Attack to foul line.
3. Slide to sideline.
4. Slide across the court.
5. Slide back to lane.
6. Retreat to baseline.
7. Slide to corner and 10 pushups.
8. Get back in line and rest up.

*25 seconds each — allow no lousy slides.

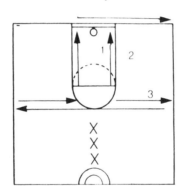

Diagram 1

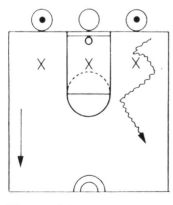

Diagram 2

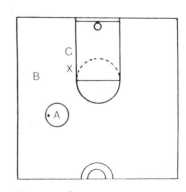

Diagram 3

Diagram 2 — Drill 2 — Zig Zag 2½-3 Minutes.

Diagram 3 — Drill 3 — Post Defense — When ball is above foul line extended, play on the high side of the post.

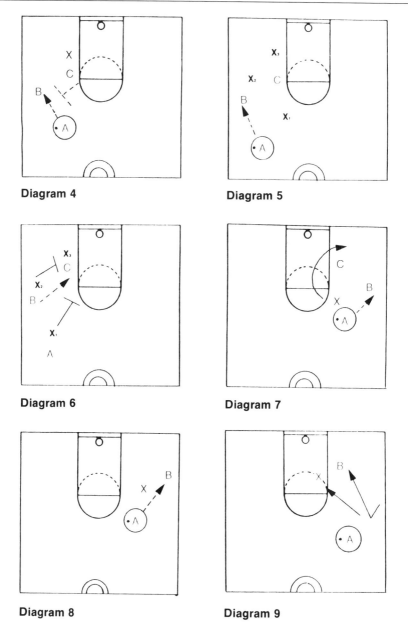

Diagram 4 — When the ball is passed below the foul line we play on the low side of the post man.

Diagram 5 — Drill 4 — Post Defense. As ball moves from A to B, we pressure B, jump to ball from A and play the low side of C.

Diagram 6 — Post Defense. Defensive post man tries to stay

DEFENSIVE DRILLS

between man and basket. The 2 outside men jam down on post. We gamble — the ball is only 8'-9' feet away.

Diagram 7 — Drill 6 — Defensive Post. If C is 15' feet away we allow the defensive post to slide behind as the ball is passed from A to B.

Diagram 8 — Drill 7 — Contesting Pass. Get lead foot up in land and get close to B. Ignore his first step to the basket — stay closed until he gets to lane.

Diagram 9 — Drill 7 — (Cont.) Open up and get in a "ball-you-man" position in the lane.

Diagram 10 — Drill 8 — 2 man contesting X2 can't allow a pass to B between wing and key area.

Diagram 11 — Drill 9 — 3 man contesting X2 and X3 contest and get on ball side of lane to HELP!

Diagram 12 — Drill 10 — 3 man contesting this is too far for X2 to contest pass to B so X1 MUST STOP REVERSAL.

Diagram 13A — Jump to the ball — X1 jumps to the ball and stays below A to stop his cut to the basket. X1 should have his hand in the passing lane (B to A) and still contest reversal. Keep ball on one side.

Diagram 10

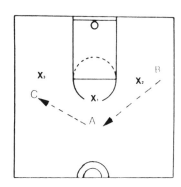

Diagram 11

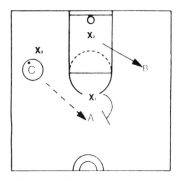

Diagram 12

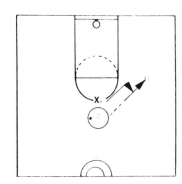

Diagram 13A

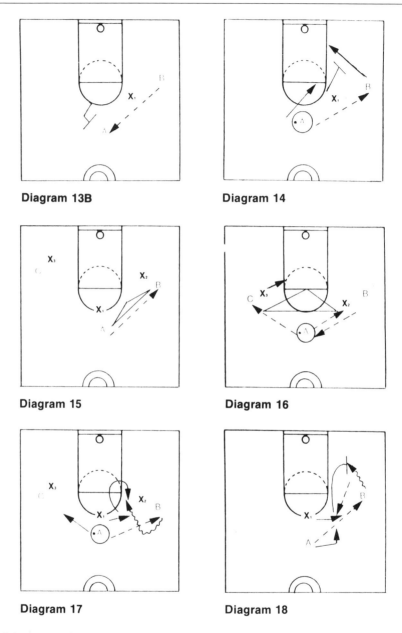

Diagram 13B — (Cont.)

Diagram 14 — Someimes X1 has to jump to the ball then jam all the way down into the lane.

Diagram 15 — Drill 12 — Flat triangle help side defense (2 man). X1 will jump to the ball and he one steps off the line of the ball.

Diagram 16 — Drill 13 — Rotate the ball and don't contest the pass back to the point. Work on contesting the wings and help position.

DEFENSIVE DRILLS

Diagram 17 — Drill 14 — Help and Recover.
X1 jumps in the direction of the ball on pass from A to B. As A moves X1 stays one step below him and helps out as B drives past X2. It's ball-you-man, flat triangles, and help and recover.

Diagram 18 — This is help on the guard to forward pass. B penetrates and X1 helps. B passes back to A and X1 has to recover to be in good position.

Diagram 19 — The pass goes guard to guard, X1 jumps to the ball. The guard penetrates and X1 helps. The guard passes back and X1 must recover and be in good position.

Diagram 20 — Drill 17 — Driving Drills. X1 plays to B's inside to force his drive to the corner. B will have less scoring and passing opportunities.

Diagram 21 — If B is allowed to drive the middle he has more options and a better shot.

Diagram 22 — If B turns the corner to drive the baseline then the defensive post will pick him up. The ball went below the foul line so the defense post is on low side.

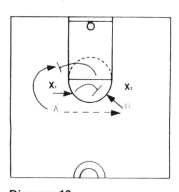
Diagram 19

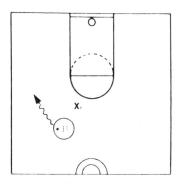
Diagram 20

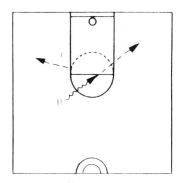
Diagram 21

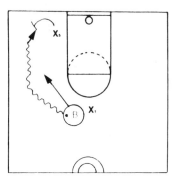
Diagram 22

Diagram 23 — Drill 18 — X1 works to get B to stop his dribble and then jumps to his highside to keep B from reversing the ball.

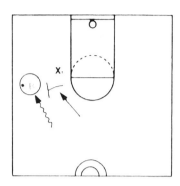

Diagram 23